CW01631559

BRANCH LINES TO SKEGNESS AND MABLETHORPE

also to Spilsby and Coningsby

Vic Mitchell and Keith Smith

MP Middleton Press

Front cover: Although opened as a Light Railway, Tumby Woodside had conventional signalling and level crossing gates. They are seen on 27th April 1970, as a class 105 DMU departs east. (Colour-Rail.com)

Back cover: 1947 Railway Clearing House map.

Published January 2016

ISBN 978 1 908174 84 0

© *Middleton Press, 2016*

Design Deborah Esher
Typesetting Cassandra Morgan

Published by
Middleton Press
Easebourne Lane
Midhurst
West Sussex
GU29 9AZ
Tel: 01730 813169
Email: info@middletonpress.co.uk
www.middletonpress.co.uk

Printed in the United Kingdom by Henry Ling Limited, at the Dorset Press, Dorchester, DT1 1HD

CONTENTS

ACKNOWLEDGEMENTS

We are very grateful for the assistance received from many of those mentioned in the credits, also from M.Back, J.Bonsall, A.J.Castledine, G.Croughton, G.Gartside, F.Hornby, S.C.Jenkins, N.Langridge, B.Lewis, J.P.McCrickard, A.C.Mott, Mr D. and Dr. S.Salter, T.Walsh and our supportive families.

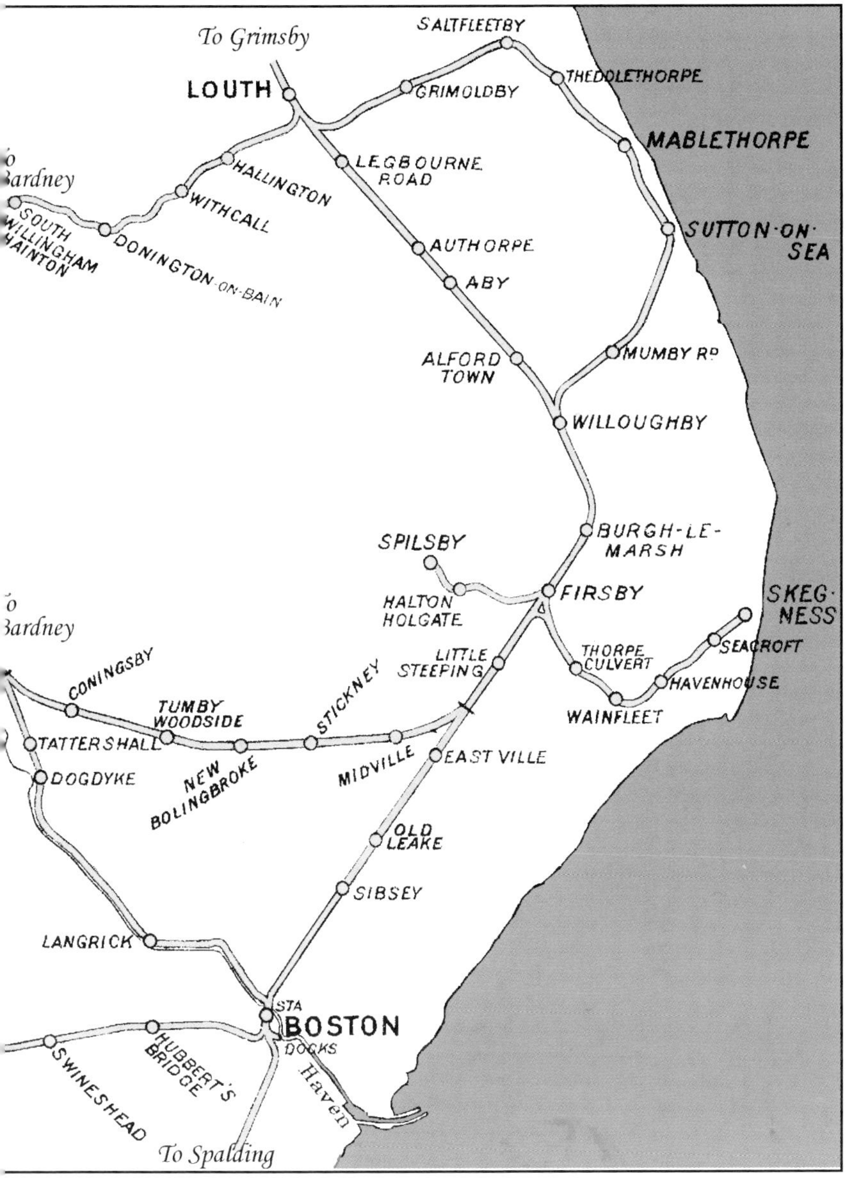

I. 1947 Railway Clearing House map.

INDEX

GEOGRAPHICAL SETTING

All the lines in this album are between the North Sea coast and the Lincolnshire Wolds. This is a ridge of high ground, which joins the Cotswold Hills of Somerset with the North Yorkshire Moors. There is a notable gap created by the River Humber.

The first line herein is fairly level and traverses an area which is mainly on chalk and flanked to the west by sand and clay.

The second route climbs gently up the valley of the Steeping River, which is at the eastern edge of an area reclaimed from peat bogs and salt marshes.

Our third journey is over East Fen and is thus over level agricultural land, which has high productivity figures.

The Skegness branch also runs close to the Steeping River and through a fertile district often termed the "bread basket of England". Nearing the popular holiday resort at the terminus, the line passes over Croft Marsh.

The maps are to the scale of 25ins to 1 mile, with north at the top, unless otherwise indicated.

The historical quotations are from Bradshaw's Guide of 1866.

HISTORICAL BACKGROUND

The main line from which all the branches diverge opened in stages during 1848, linking Peterborough with Grimsby. It was built by the East Lincolnshire Railway under an Act of June 1846 and operated by the Great Northern Railway. It was double track from the outset. The later branches were also worked by the GNR.

The first was created by the Spilsby & Firsby Railway under an Act of 1865 and opened on 1st May 1868. It became part of the GNR in 1891.

Next came the Wainfleet & Firsby Railway, which came into use on 24th October 1871. It was extended to Skegness on 28th July 1873 and was absorbed by the GNR in 1896.

Following on was the Louth & East Coast Railway, which came into use between Louth and Mablethorpe on 17th October 1877. It became GNR property in 1908. Louth received trains from Bardney from 1876.

The Sutton & Willoughby Railway obtained its Act in July 1884 and carried passengers from 4th October 1886. It was extended to Mablethorpe on 14th July 1888 and became part of the GNR in 1902.

The Coningsby Loop was authorised under the 1896 Light Railways Act and was opened by the GNR on 1st January 1913. The latter became part of the London & North Eastern Railway upon the railway grouping of 1923.

The first passenger closure was the Spilsby branch, which took place on 11th September 1939. Nationalisation came in 1948 and the district became part of the Eastern Region of British Railways.

All stations closed between Louth and Mablethorpe on 5th December 1960 and between the latter and Willoughby on 5th October 1970. The Coningsby Loop lost all traffic on the same day. Goods withdrawal dates are given in the captions.

The Skegness services were privatised on 2nd March 1997, the main line north from Firsby to Grimsby having closed in 1970. They were operated by Central Trains until 11th November 2007, when East Midlands Trains took over.

PASSENGER SERVICES

Mablethorpe Loop

Back in 1878, there were six departures from Louth through to Willoughby on weekdays. We have found no evidence of Sunday services on this section. By 1889, there were just two through trains, with three more working the extremities, although most overlapped providing six services between Sutton-on-Sea and Mablethorpe.

This did not persist and by 1922 there were just four through trains, plus one more on the southern part, which was the busiest section. Similar figures applied up to World War II. By 1944, there were only three trains, with extras running on the southern part.

In 1960, the final summer of the northern section, there were diesel trains operating eight trips over the full length of the loop. Passenger traffic was booming and there were many extras south of Mablethorpe, particularly on Saturdays. There were even two on Sundays.

In the final year of the southern section, 1970, there were nine trips each weekday.

Spilsby Branch

Some times are included in the first two tables shown herein. Most timetables throughout the life of the line showed six return trips, weekdays only. There was occasionally one train on Sundays.

Coningsby Loop

The main purpose of the route was to provide a shorter journey between the Midlands and the East Coast holiday resorts and thus many of the trains were non-stop expresses. Double track was provided from the outset.

There were four or five stopping trains in most years, on weekdays, but very few on Sundays. In 1965-70, they were reduced to three, but there were three more between Lincoln and Tumby Woodside for these final few years of "The New Line", as it was known.

Skegness Branch

The 1889 timetable is included as an example of the simple service provided in the first decade; but none ran on Sundays. We jump to 1924 to show the complex connections and through coaches that were provided after World War I, when holidays were possible again. We can then study the 1948 issue, after the next war, when traffic was approaching its peak.

In June 1960, branch trains numbered ten (four on Sundays). From beyond Firsby, there were seven (plus two Sundays only). The arrivals numbered 15 on weekdays in 2013, with nine on summer Sundays.

July 1878

BOSTON, FIRSBY, SPILSBY, SKEGNESS, BURGH, ALFORD, LOUTH, MABLETHORPE, and GRIMSBY.—Great Northern. **Sndys.**

Kings Cross Sta.,	aft	mrn	mrn	mrn	mrn	mrn	1,2,3	aft	aft	aft	aft	aft	aft	aft	aft (Sndys.)	mrn (Sndys.)	aft (Sndys.)
124 London dep	9e0	....	....	5 15	....	....	9 0	....	....	....	....	2 45	....	....	9 0	7 30	....
132 Peterbro' ,,	2 30	....	....	6 55	8 15	....	1057	....	....	....	....	4 30	....	....	2 30	1050	....
Boston ....dep	3 30	....	6 30	8 20	9 45	....	1235	....	3 25	....	5 0	6 5	....	....	3 30	2 0	....
Sibsey	mrn	....	6 40	8 30	b	....	1244	....	3 35	....	5 10	6 14	....	....	mrn	2 10	....
Old Leake........	....	....	6 45	8 35	b	....	....	....	3 40	....	5 15	6 19	....	....	....	2 16	....
East Ville........	....	....	6 54	8 44	b	....	1254	....	3 49	....	5 23	6 27	....	....	....	2 25	....
Little Steeping.	....	....	7 2	8 53	b	....	....	....	3 58	....	b	6 35	....	....	....	2 34	....
Firsby ......arr	4 0	....	7 7	9 0	1020	....	1 6	....	4 8	┐	5 33	6 42	....	....	4 0	2 40	....
Firsby ..dep	1,2,3 class.	....	7 20	9c 5	1023	1112	1 10		Wednesdays only.	4 7	Except Wednesdays.	6 46	6 11	....	1,2,3 class. Sunday Train.	....	8 25
Haltn Holgate		....	b	b	b	b	b			b		b	....	....		....	8 30
Spilsby ..arr		....	7 35	9c20	1035	1127	1 25			4 22		7 1	6 21	....		....	8 38
Firsby ...dep		....	7 25	9 7	Wednesdays only.	1118	1 12	Wednesdays only.		4 14		6 48	Stop	9 25		2 45	....
Thorpe Culvrt		....	b	b		b	b			b		b		b		b	aft
Wainfleet....		6 8	7 40	9 21		1138	1 25			4 27		7 1	....	9 35		3 0	6 0
Croftbank ..		b	b	b		b	b			b		b	....	Extra.—Firsby to Spilsby on Tuesdays and Thursdays at 9 27 aft.		b	b
Cowbank		b	b	b		b	b			b		b	....			b	b
Skegness..arr		6 23	8 0	9 35		1155	1 40			4 42		7 15	....			3 15	6 15
Firsby ....dep	4 1	....	7 9	9 2		Stop	1 8		4 10	Stop	5 35	6 44	....		4 1	2 42	....
Burgh	4 6	....	7 15	9 7			1 14		4 15		5 40	6 49	....		4 6	2 48	....
Willoughby....	....	....	7 23	9 16		....	1 24	☞	4 25	....	5 48	6 57	....		....	2 57	....
Alford	4 20	....	7 31	9 26		....	1 32		4 35	....	5 58	7 4	....		4 20	3 5	....
Claythorpe	....	....	7 39	9 32		....	1 40		4 39	....	6 6	7 11	....		....	3 12	....
Authorpe........	....	....	b	9 37		....	d		4 46	....	6 11	7 16	....		....	3 16	....
Legbourne	....	....	7 50	9 45	non	....	....		4 56	aft	6 19	7 23	aft		....	3 25	....
Louth (see below)	4 38	....	8 0	9 56	12 0	non	1 57	3 50	5 9	┘	6 27	7 31	8 0		4 38	3 33	....
Louth....dep	....	....	8 10	1020	....	12 0	3 10			5 25	....	8 10	....		....	Sundy Train.	....
Grimoldby ..	....	....	8 20	1030	....	1210	3 20			5 35	....	8 20	....		....		....
Saltfleetby ..	....	....	8 33	1043	....	1223	3 33			5 48	....	8 31	....		....		....
Theddlethrpe	....	....	8 40	1050	....	1230	3 40			5 55	....	8 36	....		....		....
Mablethrpe a	....	....	8 50	11 0	....	1240	3 50			6 5	....	8 45	....		....		....
Ludborough....	....	....	8 12	1015	12 9	....	....	4 0	5 32	....	6 39	f	8 10		....	3 45	....
North Thoresby	....	....	8 17	1020	1214	....	2 14	4 5	5 37	....	6 44	f	8 15		....	3 51	....
Holton-le-Clay..	....	....	8 22	1025	1219	....	....	4 10	5 42	....	6 49	f	8 20		....	3 56	....
Waltham [245	....	....	8 29	1030	1224	....	....	4 15	5 47	....	6 55	f	8 25		....	4 5	....
Gt Grimsby 250	5 0	....	8 40	1033	1232	....	2 30	4 25	5 55	....	7 5	8 0	8 33		5 0	4 15	....
Hull 250 arr	8 0	....	1030	1215	2 5	....	4 0	6 0	9 5	....	9 5	9 45	....		9 10	5 30	....

Corporation P.,	mrn	mrn	mrn	mrn	mrn	aft	aft	aft	a	aft	mrn (Sndys.)	aft (Sndys.)	a (Sndys.)
Hull 250 dep	....	....	8 0	9 30	....	1210	....	3 10	6 35	....	8 15	....	5 40
Gt. Grimsby dep	6 50	7 25	9 35	11 0	....	2 20	3 0	4 40	8 13	....	9 40	....	7 15
Waltham	b	7 32	9 42	11 7	....	2 26	3 7	4 47	1,2,3 class	....	9 48	....	aft
Holton-le-Clay..	b	7 37	9 48	1112	....	2 31	3 12	4 52		....	9 54	....	1,2,3 class.
North Thoresby	6 10	7 43	9 54	1118	....	2 37	3 18	4 59		....	10 2	....	
Ludborough....	b	7 49	9 59	1124	....	2 41	3 24	5 4		....	10 7	....	
Mablethrpe d	....	....	9 5	Weds. only.	1110	2 5	....	4 20	7 10	9 0	....	....	....
Theddlethrpe	....	....	9 14		1120	2 15	....	4 29	7 20	9 8	....	....	....
Saltfleetby ..	....	....	9 21		1127	2 22	....	4 35	7 27	9 13	....	....	....
Grimoldby ..	....	....	9 34		1137	2 35	....	4 47	7 37	9 23	....	....	....
Louth (see below)		....	9 47		1150	2 46	....	5 1	7 59	9 35	....	....	....
Louth (see below)	6 27	8 0	1016	1135	....	3 0	3 35	5 21	8 40	Stop	1020	....	7 42
Legbourne	b	Stop	1023	Stop	....	3 8	}	5 27	....	Tues. & Thurs. only.	1027	....	....
Authorpe......	b		1031		....	3 16	☞ Wednesdays only.	5 33	....		1035	....	....
Claythorpe	6 44	....	1036	....	....	3 21		5 38	....		1040	....	....
Alford	6 52	....	1047	....	....	3 30		5 48	9 0		1050	....	8 2
Willoughby	6 59	..	1055	....	....	3 39		5 54	....		11 0	....	....
Burgh	7 7	....	11 4	....	....	3 47		6 1	9 12		11 7	....	3 14
Firsby......arr	7 12	mrn	11 9	aft	....	3 54		6 7	9 18		1112	....	3 19
Skegness dep	6 35	8 25	1026	1226	....	3 7		5 30	8 40		....	5 30	7 40
Cowbank	b	b	b	b	....	b		b	b		....	b	b
Croftbank ..	b	b	b	b	....	b		b	b		....	b	b
Wainfleet ..	6 50	8 37	1035	1244	....	3 27		5 45	8 55	☞	....	5 45	7 55
Thorpe Culvrt	b	b	b	b	....	b		b	b		....		b
Firsby....arr	7 2	8 52	1052	1 0	....	3 42	aft	6 0	9 10	}	....	aft	8 10
Spilsby ..dep	6 45	8 37	1042	1245	....	3 37	6 26	5 42	....	8 50	....	2 20	....
Haltn Holgate	6 50	8 42	1047	1250	....	3 42	b	5 47	....	b	....	2 25	....
Firsby....arr	7 0	8 55	11 0	1 5	....	3 53	6 39	5 58	....	9 5	....	2 35	....
Firsby ....dep	7 15	9 0	1112	....	....	3 58	....	6 10	9 20	....	1115	....	8 20
Little Steeping.	7 21	9 5	1118	....	....	4 3	....	6 15	....	....	1120	....	....
East Ville......	7 28	9 13	1126	....	....	4 10	....	6 23	....	....	1129	....	....
Old Leake......	7 36	9 20	1134	....	....	4 19	....	6 30	....	....	1140	....	....
Sibsey ..[*below*	7 42	9 25	1140	....	....	4 23	....	6 35	....	....	1144	....	....
Boston 132 *and*	7 55	9 35	1153	....	....	4 35	....	6 47	9 47	....	12 0	....	8 46
132 Peterbro' a	9 35	....	1 25	....	....	6 5	....	8 5	1046	....	4 35	....	9 45
127 London ..,,	1145	....	3 25	....	....	8 0	....	10 0	3 10	....	7 35	....	3 10

Boston, Alford,

a London Passengers may remain at Peterbro' all night and go forward next morning **b** Stop by signal to take up, and set down on informing the Guard at the preceding *stopping* Station. *c* Except Wednesdays from Firsby to Spilsby. **d** Stops on Tuesdays to set down from Alford; and on Fridays, when required, to take up for Louth. **e** Leaves at 8 20 aft. on Sundays. **f** Stops to set down London Passengers.

LOUTH, MABLETHORPE, SUTTON-ON-SEA, and WILLOUGHBY.—Great Northern.

Mls	Up.		mrn	mrn	mrn	aft	aft	aft	aft	aft
—	Louth	dep	8 3	....	1020	12 5	....	3 10	5 32	....
4¼	Grimoldby		8 12	....	1029	1214	....	3 20	5 42	....
8	Saltfleetby		8 24	....	1037	1222	....	3 29	5 51	....
10	Theddlethorpe		8 31	....	1042	1227	....	3 35	5 56	....
12¾	Mablethorpe	arr	8 38	....	1048	1233	....	3 41	6 2	....
		dep	8 44	1025	1050	1238	3 13	3 43	....	6 25
15½	Sutton-on-Sea	arr	8 49	1031	1055	1244	3 18	3 49	....	6 31
		dep	8 50	1032	....	1245	3 20	....	....	6 32
19½	Mumby Road		9 0	1040	....	1253	3 28	....	....	6 40
22½	Willoughby (see side)	a	9 8	1046	....	1259	3 33	....	....	6 46

Mls	Down.		mrn	mrn	mrn	aft	aft	aft	aft
—	Willoughby	dep	....	9 18	1055	1 15	4 29	....	7 8
3	Mumby Road		....	9 24	11 1	1 21	4 35	....	7 14
7	Sutton-on-Sea	arr	....	9 32	11 9	1 29	4 42	....	7 22
		dep	8 50	9 34	1111	1 31	4 43	6 40	7 24
9¾	Mablethorpe	arr	8 55	9 40	1117	1 37	4 48	6 45	7 30
		dep	9 0	....	1120	1 40	4 49	6 47	....
12½	Theddlethorpe		9 6	....	1126	1 45	4 53	6 52	....
14½	Saltfleetby		9 16	....	1131	1 50	4 58	6 58	....
18¼	Grimoldby		9 27	....	1140	1 58	5 6	7 7	....
22½	Louth 176, and at side		9 40	....	1150	2 10	5 17	7 17	....

May 1889

Boston, Spilsby, Skegness,

BOSTON, SPILSBY, SKEGNESS, LOUTH, and GRIMSBY.—Great Northern.

Miles from Boston.	Down.	Week Days. aft	mrn	mrn	mrn	mrn	aft	mrn	mrn	aft	aft	aft	aft	aft		Sundays. aft	mrn	
	King's Crss Sta.,																	
	154 London dep	1040	c	5 15	Mondays only.	....	....	....	8 50	....	1230	....	3 0	5 45	....	1040	8 35	....
	172 Petrbro "	2 30	....	6 55		8 0	....	....	1048	....	2 15	....	4 45	7 30	....	2 30	1158	....
	180 Leicester "	....	....	....		....	....	....	9 5	....	....	....	....	3 50	....	....	....	....
	169 Nottnghm "	....	....	5 30		....	....	....	1012	....	....	....	....	5 0	....	....	....	....
—	Boston......dep	3 32	6 30	8 20		9 45	Mons. only.	1030	1220	....	3 30	....	6 1	8 47	....	3 32	2 0	....
4¾	Sibsey	mrn	6 39	8 29		Sig.		e	1229	....	3 39	....	6 10	d	....	mrn	2 9	....
6½	Old Leake	....	6 44	8 34		Sig.		....	1233	....	3 44	....	6 15	f	....	....	2 14	....
9¾	East Ville	....	6 52	8 42		Sig.		e	1239	....	3 52	....	6 23	9 4	....	....	2 22	....
13	Little Steeping	....	7 0	8 51		Sig.		....	b	....	Sig.	....	6 31	f	....	....	2 31	....
15½	Firsby......arr	4 0	7 10	9 0		1020		11 0	1251	....	4 10	....	6 39	9 14	....	4 0	2 40	...
—	Firsby ...dep	....	7 15	9 g 5	1013	1023		1115	1257		4 15	6 6	6 44	....	....	....	....	....
18	Halton Holgte	....	Sig.	Sig.	Sig.	Sig.		Sig.	Sig.		Sig.	....	Sig.	....	....	....	....	....
19½	Spilsby ..arr	....	7 30	9g20	1028	1035		1130	1 10		4 30	6 16	6 59	....	....	....	....	....
—	Firsby ...dep	....	7 20	9 7	....	Wednesdays only.	Wednesdays only.	1115	1255	Wednesdays only.	4 13	....	6 46	....	....	....	....	....
17¾	Thorpe Culvrt	....	Sig.	Sig.	....			Sig.	Sig.		Sig.	....	Sig.	....	....	....	....	....
19½	Wainflet 6 8	....	7 35	9 21	....			1130	1 8		4 25	....	6 59	....	....	....	....	....
21½	Croftbnk Sig.	....	Sig.	Sig.	....			Sig.	Sig.		Sig.	....	Sig.	....	....	....	....	....
23½	Cowbank Sig.	....	Sig.	Sig.	....			Sig.	Sig.		Sig.	....	Sig.	....	....	....	....	....
24¾	Skegnss a 6 20	....	7 50	9 35	....			1145	1 23		4 38	....	7 16	....	....	....	....	....
—	Firsby .....dep	4 1	7 12	9 2	....			....	1253		4 12	....	6 42	9 17	....	4 1	2 42	....
17½	Burgh ....[side	4 6	7 18	9 7	....			....	1259		4 18	....	6 47	9 21	....	4 6	2 48	....
20¾	Willoughby, see	....	7 26	9 14	....			....	1 6		4 26	....	6 54	Sig.	....	....	2 57	....
22¼	Alford..[thorpe	4 20	7 33	9 22	....			....	1 12		4 34	....	7 0	9 33	....	4 20	3 5	....
26½	Aby, for Clay-	....	7 40	9 28	....			....	1 20		4 42	....	7 7	f j	....	....	3 12	....
27¾	Authorpe	....	7 45	9 33	....			....	1 25		4 47	....	7 12	f	....	....	3 16	....
31	Legbourne Road	....	7 53	9 41	....			....	Sig.		4 55	....	7 19	f	....	....	3 25	....
33¾	Louth (see side) arr	4 38	8 1	9 51	....			....	1 37		5 5	....	7 27	9 51	....	4 38	3 33	....
	dep	4 40	8 2	10 5	....		1210	....	1 40	3 50	5 20	....	7 29	9 53	....	4 40	3 35	....
39	Ludborough	....	8 12	1015	....		1219	....	Fri.	4 0	5 30	....	7 39	f i	....	....	3 45	....
40½	North Thoresby	....	8 17	1020	....		1224	....	1 54	4 5	5 35	....	7 43	10 6	....	....	3 51	....
42½	Holton-le-Clay	....	8 22	1025	....		1229	....	Fri.	4 10	5 40	....	7 48	f	....	....	3 56	....
44¾	Waltham..[328	....	8 31	1032	....		1236	....	2 4	4 17	5 47	....	7 54	1014	....	....	4 7	....
47¾	GtGrimsby 327	5 0	8 40	1038	....		1242	....	2 10	4 25	5 54	....	8 0	1020	....	5 0	4 15	....
—	Hull 328 arr	7 50	1025	1210	....	....	2 10	....	3 50	5 55	7 0	....	9 45	....	....	9 5	5 50	....

a London Passengers may remain at Peterbro all night and go forward next morning. **b** Stops on Wednesdays when required. *c* Leaves at 8 30 aft. on Sundays. **d** Stops when required to set down from Spalding and Stations South of Spalding. **e** Stops to take up for Firsby and Spilsby. **f** Stops when required to set down from London. *g* Except Wednesdays. *h* Arrives at 10 40 mrn. on Mondays. **i** Stops on Saturdays to set down. **j** Stops on Saturdays to set down from Alford.

May 1889

KIRKSTEAD, LITTLE STEEPING, and FIRSBY.—Great Northern.

Miles.	Week Days only.	mrn (Thro' Trn, Lincoln to Skegness, see pp. 395 & 406.)	mrn (Thro' Express, Sheffield to Skegness, Sutton-on-Sea & Mablethorpe, see pages 693, 395, and 406.)	mrn (Thro' Train, Lincoln to Skegness, see page 395.)	aft (Thro' Trn, Lincoln to Skegness, see pp. 395 & 406.)	aft (Thro' Train, Lincoln to Skegness, see page 395.)	
	Victoria Station,						
	693 Sheffield.......dep.	6 35	8 35	8 57	2 0	4 32	....
	395 Lincoln (High St.) "	9 15	9 44	11 5	4 0	5 55	....
—	Kirkstead..........dep.	9 39	10 9	1130	4 25	6 19	....
4¼	Coningsby	9 48	....	1139	4 34	6 28	....
7	Tumby Woodside	9 56	....	1147	4 42	6 36	....
9½	New Bolingbroke	10 4	....	1155	4 50	6 44	....
11½	Stickney	10 12	....	12 3	4 58	6 52	....
14	Midville	10 20	....	1211	5 6	7 0	....
18	Little Steeping	....	....	1220	....	....	....
20	Firsby 406, 408 ....arr.	10 32	1053	1225	5 18	7 12	....
29¼	406 Skegness........arr.	10 53	1114	1245	5 43	7 34	....
36½	406 Mablethorpe.... "	11 13	....	1 25	7u40	7b54	....

Miles.	Week Days only.	mrn (Thro' Train, Skegness to Lincoln, see page 394.)	aft (Thro' Trn, Skegness to Lincoln, see pp. 408 & 394.)	aft (Thro' Train, Skegness to Lincoln, see page 394.)	aft (Thro' Express, Skegness, Sutton-on-Sea, and Mablethorpe to Sheffield, see pp. 409, 394, and 702.)	aft (Thro' Trn, Skegness to Lincoln, see pp. 409 & 394.)
	408 Mablethorpe....dep.	....	1236	3 10	5 55	5 55
	408 Skegness......... "	8 25	1 25	4 0	6 10	6 25
—	Firsby..............dep.	....	1 45	4 20	6 29	6 48
2	Little Steeping	8 50	1 50	4 25	....	....
6	Midville	8 59	1 59	4 34	....	7 0
8½	Stickney	9 7	2 7	4 42	....	7 8
10½	New Bolingbroke	9 15	2 15	4 50	....	7 16
13	Tumby Woodside	9 23	2 23	4 58	....	7 24
15¾	Coningsby	9 31	2 31	5 6	....	7 32
20	Kirkstead 394......arr.	9 40	2 40	5 15	7 13	7 41
35½	394 Lincoln (High St.) arr.	10 7	3 10	5 43	7 39	8 9
78	698 Sheffield (Vic.). "	1221	4z52	7 47	8 53	1016

b Fridays and Saturdays. *u* Arrives at 7 20 aft. on Fridays and Saturdays. *z* Commences on 14th instant.

July 1914

WOODHALL JUNCTION, LITTLE STEEPING, and FIRSBY.

Miles		Week Days mn	R x	mrn x	xb S	mrn b	aft x	aft x	aft x	Suns. mrn	mrn x
	887 Lincoln (LNE) dp	755	9 15	9 L15	1115	1120	1215	415	6 0	8 51	10 51
—	Woodhall Junc. dep.	847	9 41	9 L41	1143	1147	1239	450	629	9 39	11 17
4¼	Coningsby	855	....	9 L49	....	1154	....	457	636	....	11 24
7	Tumby Woodside	9 0	....	....	....	1159	....	5 2	641	....	....
9¼	New Bolingbroke	9 5	....	9 L57	....	12 4	....	5 7	646	....	11 32
11¼	Stickney	910	....	10 L 2	....	12 9	....	512	651	9 56	11 37
14	Midville	915	....	....	....	1214	....	517	656	10 1	11 45
18	Little Steeping	923	....	....	....	1222	....	525	7 4	....	....
20	Firsby 888 above arr.	928	....	10 L14	1218	1227	....	530	7 9	....	...
29¼	888 Skegness... arr.	957	1025	10 L42	1246	1 8	1 24	556	743	....	12 12

	Week Days mrn	mrn x	aft x	aft x	xb S	aft xb	aft x	x R	aft b	Suns. aft	aft x
Skegness .....dep.	6 35	8 0	1250	2 55	3 46	3 20	6 20	7 15	....	....	7 0
Firsby ....dep.	7 25	8 40	1 13	....	4 10	4 31	6 50	....	8 40	....	....
Little Steeping	7 30	8 45	1 18	....	....	4 36	6 55	....	....	....	....
Midville	7 38	8 53	1 26	....	....	4 44	7 4	....	....	6 22	7 26
Stickney	7 43	8 58	1 31	....	....	4 49	7 10	....	....	6 28	7 31
New Bolingbroke	7 48	9 3	1 36	....	....	4 54	7 16	....	....	....	7 36
Tumby Woodside	7 53	9 8	1 41	....	....	4 59	7 24	....	....	....	....
Coningsby	7 58	9 13	1 46	....	....	5 4	7 29	....	....	....	7 44
Woodhall Jnc. 887 arr.	8 5	9 20	1 53	3 41	4 41	5 11	7 36	8 0	9 8	6 44	7 51
887 Lincoln (LNE) arr.	9 7	9 59	2 22	4 7	5 9	5 43	8 3	8 25	9 35	7 32	8 18

b Thro Trains between Lincoln and Sutton-on-Sea & Mablethorpe pages 888 and *above*.
L 10 mins. later on Weds. and Sats.
R Weds. and Sats.
S Sats. only
x Through Trains between Lincoln and Skegness.

August 1934

NOTES — **S** Sats. only

LOUTH, MABLETHORPE, SUTTON-ON-SEA, and WILLOUGHBY.

Miles	Up.		Week Days. mrn	mrn	mrn	non	aft	aft	aft S	Suns.
—	Louth	dep.	7 42	..	9 51	..	3 3	5 47	7 29	..
4¼	Grimoldby		7 51	....	10 0	....	3 12	5 56	7 38	....
8	Saltfleetby		7 59	..	10 8	..	3 20	6 4	7 46	..
10	Theddlethorpe		8 4	....	1013	....	3 25	6 9	7 51	....
12½	Mablethorpe	arr.	8 10	..	1019	..	3 31	6 15	7 57	..
		dep.	8 13	9 25	1022	12 0	3 34	6 17	7 59	....
15½	Sutton-on-Sea	arr.	8 18	9 30	1027	12 5	3 39	6 22	8 4	..
		dep.	8 19	9 33	....	12 7	3 41	6 23	....	....
19½	Mumby Road		8 27	9 41	..	1215	3 49	6 31	..	..
22½	Willoughby 888, 890	arr.	8 33	9 47	....	1221	3 55	6 37	....	....

December 1938

BOSTON, FIRSBY, SKEGNESS, WILLOUGHBY. LOUTH, and GRIMSBY TOWN.

Week Days.

Miles from Boston.	Down.	mrn	mrn	mrn	mrn	mrn	mrn	mrn	mrn	mrn
	887 London (King's C.) dep.	1 10					4 45			7C25
	887 Peterbro' (N'th) "	3 10					6 45			8F49
	844 Leicester (Cen.). "	9LE8					4 30			7 22
	894 " A..... "									7 10
	894 Derby (Friargate) "	9E40	g						5 37	7 48
	894 Nottingham (V.). "	10E41	g				5 25		6A38	8 30
	894 Grantham....... "	1a22					6 30		7U15	9 35
—	Boston dep.	4 3					7 58			10 44
4½	Sibsey						8 7			
6¼	Old Leake						8 11			
9½	East Ville						8 17			
13	Little Steeping						8 24			
15½	Firsby 890 arr.	4 22					8 29		1014	11 3
—	Firsby dep.			7 10			8 42		1026	11 12
17½	Thorpe Culvert			7 15			8 47			11 17
19½	Wainfleet			7 21			8 52		1035	11 22
21½	Havenhouse			7 25			8 56			11 26
23½	Seacroft						a			11 31
24½	Skegness arr.			7 32			9 4		1044	11 34
—	Firsby dep.	4 25					8 36			11 5
17½	Burgh-le-Marsh	4 32					8 41			
20¾	Willoughby (below) arr.						8 48			11 14
27¾	Sutton-on-Sea arr.	8B18					9 8			11 28
31½	Mablethorpe "	8B10					9 14			11 35
—	Willoughby dep.						8 50			11N15
23¾	Alford Town	4 43					8 57			
26¼	Aby, for Claythorpe						9 3			
27¾	Authorpe						9 6			
31	Legbourne Road						9 12			
33¼	Louth 891 arr.	4 58					9 18			12N8
	Louth 891 dep.	5 4	6 40		7 43	8 30	9 21	9 57		12 20
36¼	Fotherby				7 49			10 3		a
38¼	Utterby				7 54			10 8		
39	Ludborough		6 49		7 57		9 30	1011		12 29
40½	North Thoresby	5 14	6 53		8 1		9 34	1015		12 33
41½	Grainsby				8 4			1018		
42½	Holton-le-Clay		6 58		8 8		9 39	1022		12 38
43½	Holton Village		7 1		8 11	8 44		1025		12 41
44½	Waltham		7 5		8 15	8 48	9 44	1029		12 45
46¾	Weelsby Road				8 20			1034		
47	Hainton Street [916				8 22			1036		
47½	Grimsby Town 910, arr.	5 25	7 12		8 25	8 55	9 50	1039		12 51
50½	916 Cleethorpes arr.	6 6	7 30		8 45	9 23	1027	1220		1 27
									TC from Lincoln, page 890.	TC Derby (Friargate) to Skegness

Miles from Boston.	Down.	mrn	aft	aft	aft	aft	mrn	aft	mrn	aft S	aft	aft	aft	aft	aft	aft	aft E	aft	aft
	887 London (King's C.) dep.	8 45					y1010		11 30					4 5	4*0	4 5			
	887 Peterbro' (N'th) "	1050					y1136		2 18					5 35	5 35	5 35			
	844 Leicester (Cen.). "	8 39					11 2		11 2	1 42			12u25	2P28	2P28	2P28			
	894 " A..... "	9c10								12b45			12h30						
	894 Derby (Friargate) "	8 30					1042		10 42	1 26				1 26	1 26	1 26			
	894 Nottingham (V.). "	9 38					1145		11 45	2 45			1u23	3P19	3P19	3P19			
	894 Grantham....... "	11 0					1246		1d23				2U52	4P28	4P28	4P28			
—	Boston dep.	1210					1 41		3 27	4 8				6 21	6 22	6 27		6 47	6 47
4½	Sibsey	1219							3 36									6 56	6 56
6¼	Old Leake	1223							3 40									7 0	7 0
9½	East Ville	1229							3 46									7 6	7 6
13	Little Steeping	1236							3 52				5 19					7 13	7.13
15½	Firsby 890 arr.	1241					2 0		3 57				5 24		6 40	6 45		7 19	7 19
—	Firsby dep.			1250		1 48	2 5		4 5		4 30		5 29		6 49	6 54			
17½	Thorpe Culvert					1 53			a		4 35		5 34						
19½	Wainfleet			1259		1 58	2 14		4 14	4 35	4 41		5 39		6 58	7 8			
21½	Havenhouse					2 2					4 45		5 43						
23½	Seacroft					2 7					4 50								
24½	Skegness arr.			1 8		2 10	2 23		4 23	4 44	4 53		5 50		7 7	7 12			
—	Firsby dep.	1247							4 0						6 42	6 47		7 26	7 26
17½	Burgh-le-Marsh	1252							4 4							6 52		7 31	7 31
20¾	Willoughby (below) arr.	1258							4 10						6 51	6 58		7 38	7 38
27¾	Sutton-on-Sea arr.	1 47							4 29						7 13	7 18			
31½	Mablethorpe "	1 55							4 38						7 20	7 25			
—	Willoughby dep.	1 0			1N34				4 12			4N16			6 53	7 0	7V0	7 41	7 41
23¾	Alford Town	1 7							4 18						6 58	7 6		7 48	7 48
26¼	Aby, for Claythorpe	1 13							4 24									7 56	7 56
27¾	Authorpe	1 17							4 28									7 59	7 59
31	Legbourne Road	1 23							4 34									8 5	8 5
33¼	Louth 891 arr.	1 28			2N26				4 39			5N10			7 12	7 20	7V59	8 11	8 11
	Louth 891 dep.	1 30	1 43					3 5	4 42			5 25			7 14	7 22		8 21	8 35
36¼	Fotherby							3 11				5 31							8 41
38¼	Utterby							3 16				5 36							
39	Ludborough		1 52					3 19	4 51			5 39						8 30	8 46
40½	North Thoresby		1 56					3 23	4 55			5 43						8 34	8 50
41½	Grainsby							3 26				5 46							
42½	Holton-le-Clay		2 1					3 30	5 0			5 50						8 39	8 55
43½	Holton Village		2 4					3 33				5 53						8 42	8 58
44½	Waltham		2 8					3 37	5 5			5 57			Dd	Aa		8 46	9 2
46¾	Weelsby Road							3 42				6 2							
47	Hainton Street [916							3 44				6 4							
47½	Grimsby Town 910, arr.	1 47	2 14					3 47	5 11			6 7		7 15	7 33	7 42		8 52	9 8
50½	916 Cleethorpes arr.	2 8	3 1					4 8	5 53			6*26		7 31	7 49	7 59		9 33	9 33
				TC from Lincoln page 890.			TC Grantham to Skegness.			Saturdays only. TC Nottingham to Skegness.			TC from Lincoln, page 890.	Fridays only. TC King's Cross to Cleethorpes Buffet Car.	Except Fridays Buffet Car. TC King's Cross to Cleethorpes. Except Fridays.	Fridays only. TC King's Cross to Cleethorpes. Fris. only.	Except Saturdays	Except Saturdays.	Sats. only.

BOSTON, FIRSBY, SKEGNESS, WILLOUGHBY, LOUTH, and GRIMSBY TOWN.

Down.	Week Days—continued. aft	aft	E	S	aft	aft		Sundays. mrn	mrn	mrn	aft	non	aft	aft	
887 London (K. C.)..dep.		F	5 50	5 50	7 15					9 45		12 0			
887 Peterboro' (N.). "			7 28	7 28	8 42					1123		2 9			
844 Leicester (Cen.) "		5 11			5 18							8P10			
894 " A... "			3x45	3 15											
894 Derby (Friarg'te "		4 53	3x54	3 54	4P53							11P29			
894 Nottingham (V.) "		6 0	5x0	5 0	6P14							12P12			
894 Grantham...... "			6 36	6 36	7P21							1P24			
Boston dep.		7 21	8 37	8 37	9 27					1212		3 29			
Sibsey			8 47	8 46								3 38			
Old Leake				8 50								3 42			
East Ville			Nn	8 56								3 48			
Little Steeping				9 3											
Firsby 890 arr.		7 39	9 0	9 8	9 45					1231		3 57			
Firsby dep.	7 22	7 43	9 20	9 20	9 50				1056		1240	4 5		7 55	
Thorpe Culvert	7 27		9 26	9 26					11 1		1245	4 10		8 0	
Wainfleet	7 32	7 52	9 31	9 31	9 59			9 51	11 6		1250	4 15	5 30	8 5	
Havenhouse	7 36		9 35	9 35				9 55	1110		1254	4 19	5 34	8 9	
Seacroft	7 41		9 40	9 40											
Skegness arr.	7 44	8 1	9 43	9 43	10 8			10 2	1117		1 1	4 26	5 41	8 16	
Firsby dep.			9 3	9 10	9 47					1233		4 1			
Burgh-le-Marsh			9 8	9 15								4 6			
Willoughby 888 ... arr.			9 14	9 22								4 13			
888 Sutton-on-Sea .. arr.															
888 Mablethorpe... "															
Willoughby dep.			9 15	9 23								4 21			
Alford Town			9 21	9 29						1246		4 28			
Aby, for Claythorpe												4 34			
Authorpe												4 37			
Legbourne Road															
Louth 891 arr.			9 35	9 44	1010					1 0		4 47			
Louth 891 dep.			9 39	9 48	1012	1022				1 4		4 51			
Fotherby															
Utterby															
Ludborough						1031						5 0			
North Thoresby			Yy	Yy		1035						5 4			
Grainsby															
Holton-le-Clay						1040						5 9			
Holton Village						1043									
Waltham			9 55	10 4		1047						5 14			
Weelsby Road															
Hainton Street.....[916															
Grimsby Town 910, ar.			10 1	1010	1029	105[illegible]				1K28		5 20			
916 Cleethorpes ... arr.			1032	1032	1047	1119				1 38		5 38			
	TC from Lincoln, page 890.	TC Nottingham to Skegness. Fridays only			TC and Buffet Car Peterboro to Cleethorpes	Thurs. and Sats.				Buffet Car. TC King's Cross to Cleethorpes					

NOTES.

A Belgrave Rd.
A Via Mansfield & Lincoln.
Aa Stops at 7 36 aft to set down from King's Cross.
a Stops when required. Passengers wishing to alight must inform Guard at preceding *stopping* Station.
a Via Peterboro (N.); dep. 1 5 mrn Mons
B Via Louth.
b Via Bottesford
C Via Grantham. On Weds. passengers travel via Peterboro (N.) and Spalding.
c Dep 8 56 mrn Sats.
Dd Stops 7 27 aft. to set down from King's Cross.
d Via Peterbro (N.) Dep 12 57 aft on Sats.
E or E Except Sats.
F Fridays only.
F Via Grantham. Dep 9 30 mrn on Weds via Spalding
g Via Peterbro' (N.): dep Derby 10 9 and Nottingham 11 aft. Weds., and Derby 9 7 and Nottingham 9 48 aft. Suns.
h Via Lincoln. Dep 12 45 aft Sats
K Grimsby Docks.
L Via Peterbro' (N). Dep. Leicester (C.) 8 45 aft. Suns.
N Via Mablethorpe.
Nn Stops on Weds when required to set down.
P Via Peterbro' (N.)
S or S Sats. only.
TC Thro Carriage.
U Via Lincoln.
u Sats. only. Applies only to Thorpe Culvert.
V Via Mablethorpe. Dep. Willoughby 5 mins later Fris.
x Except Fris.
Yy Stops when required to set down on notice to the Guard at Peterbro (N).
y Via Grantham.
* 5 mins. later on Sats.

December 1938

Table 71 WILLOUGHBY, SUTTON-ON-SEA, MABLETHORPE, and LOUTH

Week Days only

Miles		a.m	a.m S	a.m E	a.m VO	a.m AN	a.m	a.m SN	a.m SL	a.m BN		p.m UF	p.m AD	p.m	p.m SN	p.m		p.m		p.m E	p.m S	
	Willoughby dep	7 52	8 48	8 50	9 50	1010	11 4	1123	1133	1138	..	..	1240	..	4 33	5 0	..	7 20	..	8 10	8 10	..
3	Mumby Road	..	8 54	8 56	9 57	1017	1110	1130	1140	1145	..	..	..	..	4 40	5 6	..	..	..	Dd	Dd	..
7	Sutton-on-Sea arr	8 3	9 1	9 3	10 4	1024	1117	1137	1147	1152	..	1235	1254	..	4 47	5 13	..	7 31	..	8 23	8 23	..
	Sutton-on-Sea dep	8 5	9 2	9 4	10 7	1029	1120	1140	1155	1155	..	1238	1257	2 33	4 50	5 16	..	7 33	..	8 24	8 24	..
9½	Mablethorpe arr	8 10	9 7	9 9	1012	1034	1125	1145	12 0	12 0	..	1243	1 2	2 38	4 55	5 21	..	7 38	..	8 29	8 29	..
	Mablethorpe dep	8 15	..	..	..	..	1129	..	..	..	..	..	..	2 40	..	5 25	..	7 40	..	8 32	8 32	..
12½	Theddlethorpe	8 21	..	..	..	..	1135	..	..	..	..	..	..	..	..	5 31	..	Cc	..	8 38	8 38	..
14½	Saltfleetby	8 26	..	..	..	..	1140	..	..	..	..	..	..	..	..	5 36	..	..	..	Zz	8 43	..
18½	Grimoldby	8 35	..	..	..	..	1149	..	..	..	..	..	..	2 56	..	5 45	..	..	..	8 52	8 52	..
22½	Louth arr	8 44	..	..	..	..	1158	..	..	..	..	..	..	3 5	..	5 54	..	8 6	..	9 1	9 1	..

Week Days only

Miles		a.m		a.m	a.m. HK	a.m		a.m	a.m VO		p.m AN	p.m SN	p.m SL	p.m UF	p.m	p.m SJ	p.m		p.m BN	p.m SN	p.m	
	Louth dep	6 45	..	7 44	8 44	..	..	9 50	..	..	..	..	..	..	1 49	..	3 15	..	..	..	6 20	..
4½	Grimoldby	..	..	7 53	..	..	..	9 59	..	..	..	..	..	..	1 58	..	3 24	..	..	..	6 29	..
8	Saltfleetby	..	..	8 1	..	..	..	10 7	..	..	..	..	..	..	2 6	..	3 32	..	..	..	6 37	..
10	Theddlethorpe	..	..	8 6	..	..	..	10 12	..	..	..	..	..	..	2 11	..	3 37	..	..	..	6 42	..
13	Mablethorpe arr	7 8	..	8 12	9 5	..	..	10 18	..	..	..	..	..	..	2 17	..	3 43	..	..	..	6 48	..
	Mablethorpe dep	7 10	..	8 16	9 9	9 25	..	10 22	1147	..	1210	1 35	1 55	2 10	2 19	3 30	3 47	..	4 35	6 30	6 58	..
15½	Sutton-on-Sea arr	7 15	..	8 21	9 14	9 30	..	10 27	1152	..	1215	1 40	2 0	2 15	2 24	3 35	3 52	..	4 40	6 35	7 3	..
	Sutton-on-Sea dep	7 16	..	8 22	9 17	9 33	..	10 28	1155	..	1218	1 43	2 3	2 20	..	3 38	3 55	..	4 43	6 38	7 5	..
19½	Mumby Road	..	..	8 30	9 25	9 41	..	10 36	12 3	..	1226	1 51	2 11	..	..	..	4 4	..	4 51	6 46	..	..
22½	Willoughby arr	7 28	..	8 36	9 31	9 47	..	10 42	12 9	..	1232	1 57	2 17	..	..	..	4 10	..	4 57	6 52	7 17	..

A Saturdays only. Will not run after 15th September
B Except Saturdays. Runs 25th June to 14th September inclusive
Cc Calls at 7 46 p.m. when required to set down from Boston and beyond
D Through Train from Manchester (Cen.) dep. 8 40 a.m. (Tables 80, 65, and 68)
Dd Calls at 8 16 p.m. to set down only
E Except Saturdays
F Through Train from or to Derby (Friargate) (Table 68)
H Saturdays only. Runs 7th July to 8th September inclusive
J Through Train to Manchester (C.) arr. 8 2 p.m. (Tables 65 and 80)
K Through Train to King's Cross (Table 68)
L Through Train to or from Leicester (Belgrave Road) (Table 68)
N Through Train from or to Nottingham (Table 68)
O Through Train from or to Basford and Bulwell (Tables 2, 79, 65 and 68)
S Saturdays only
U Saturdays only. Will not run after 8th September
V Saturdays only. Runs 30th June to 8th September inclusive
Zz Calls when required to set down on notice being given to the guard at Mablethorpe

June 1951

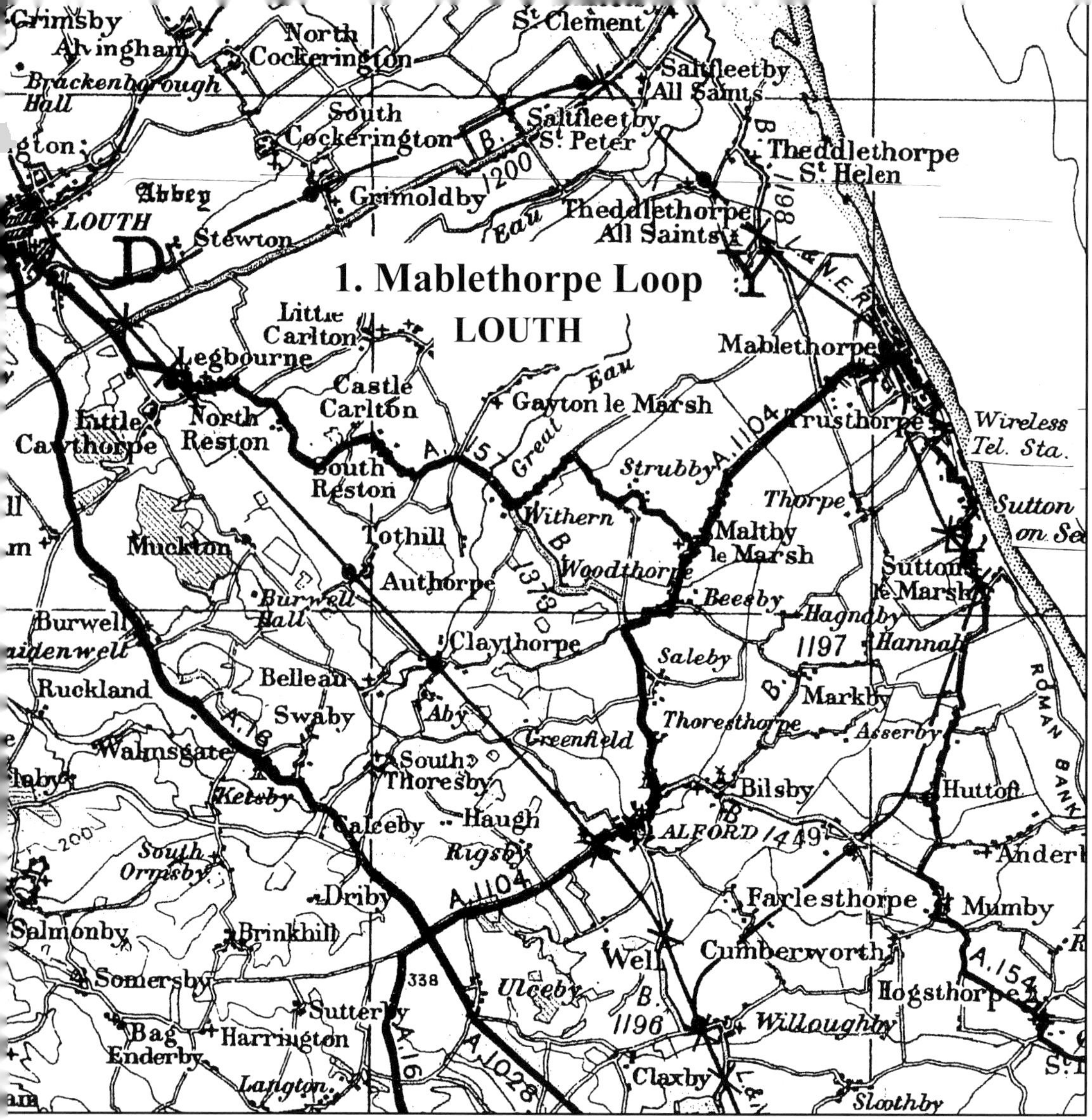

II. The 1946 edition at ¼ins to 1 mile has the main line from lower right to top left and the Loop running to the right from Louth and then towards the lower border.

1. This is a view south along the main lines, with a bay platform on the right. There was another on the opposite side at the far end. Stopping trains to Grimsby usually started from it. (Stations UK)

III. The 1897 revision is shown at 2ins to 1 mile. The branch to Mablethorpe is on the right and the route to Lincoln is on the left. Both are marked as having single tracks.

2. Steam railmotors ran between here and Grimsby from 11th December 1905, calling at a number of new halts. They were withdrawn during World War I, due to their limited capacity, but this unit lasted from 1907 until 1925. It was no. 8, built in 1906. (K.Nunn/M.Dart)

3. At the south end on 3rd July 1936 is class D3 4-4-0 no. 4314. It was based at the shed on the right, which was coded 40C from 1950 until its closure in 1956. The nearest doorway can be seen to have been bricked up and fitted with a window. (H.C.Casserley)

LOUTH SOUTH

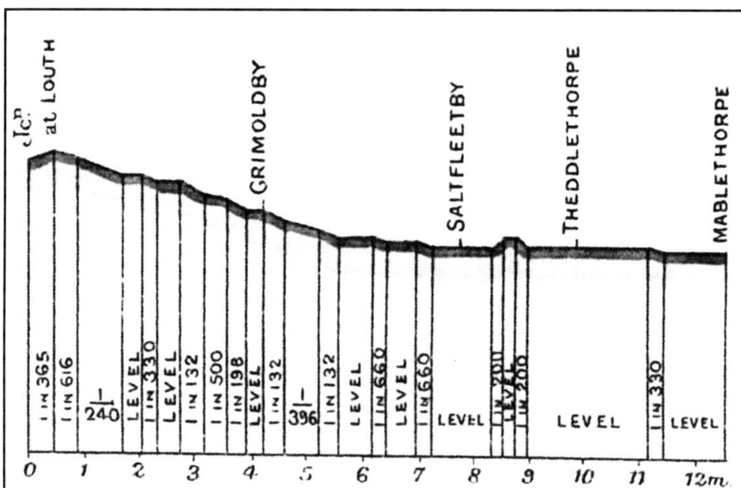
Jcn at LOUTH
GRIMOLDBY
SALTFLEETBY
THEDDLETHORPE
MABLETHORPE
1 IN 365
1 IN 616
1/240
LEVEL
1 IN 330
LEVEL
1 IN 132
1 IN 500
1 IN 198
LEVEL
1 IN 132
1/396
1 IN 132
LEVEL
1 IN 660
LEVEL
1 IN 660
LEVEL
1 IN 200
LEVEL
1 IN 200
LEVEL
1 IN 330
LEVEL
0 1 2 3 4 5 6 7 8 9 10 11 12m.

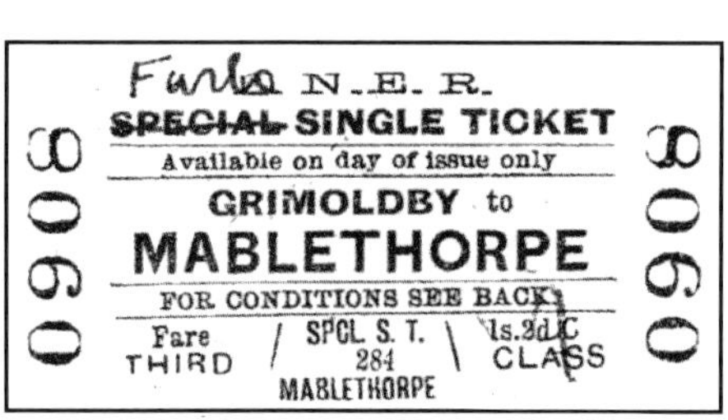
Furlo N.E.R.
SPECIAL SINGLE TICKET
Available on day of issue only
GRIMOLDBY to
MABLETHORPE
FOR CONDITIONS SEE BACK
Fare THIRD
SPCL. S. T. 284
1s.2d.C CLASS
MABLETHORPE
0908
0908

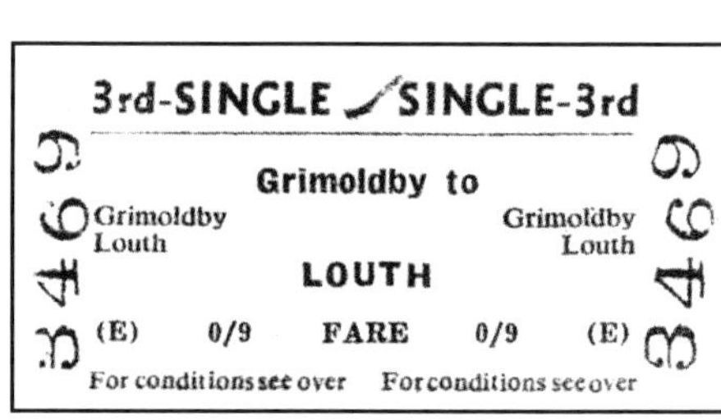
3rd-SINGLE SINGLE-3rd
Grimoldby to
Grimoldby Louth
Grimoldby Louth
LOUTH
(E) 0/9 FARE 0/9 (E)
For conditions see over For conditions see over
3469
3469

4. The single doorway at the south end of the two-road engine shed is evident in this fine panorama from 10th June 1947. Leaving the shed is class C12 4-4-2T no. 7352, while an N5 0-6-2T works in the carriage sidings. (W.A.Camwell/SLS)

5. The west elevation was recorded in July 1959, before the decade of mass motoring began in the 1960s. The style was described as neo-Jacobean. (Milepost 92½)

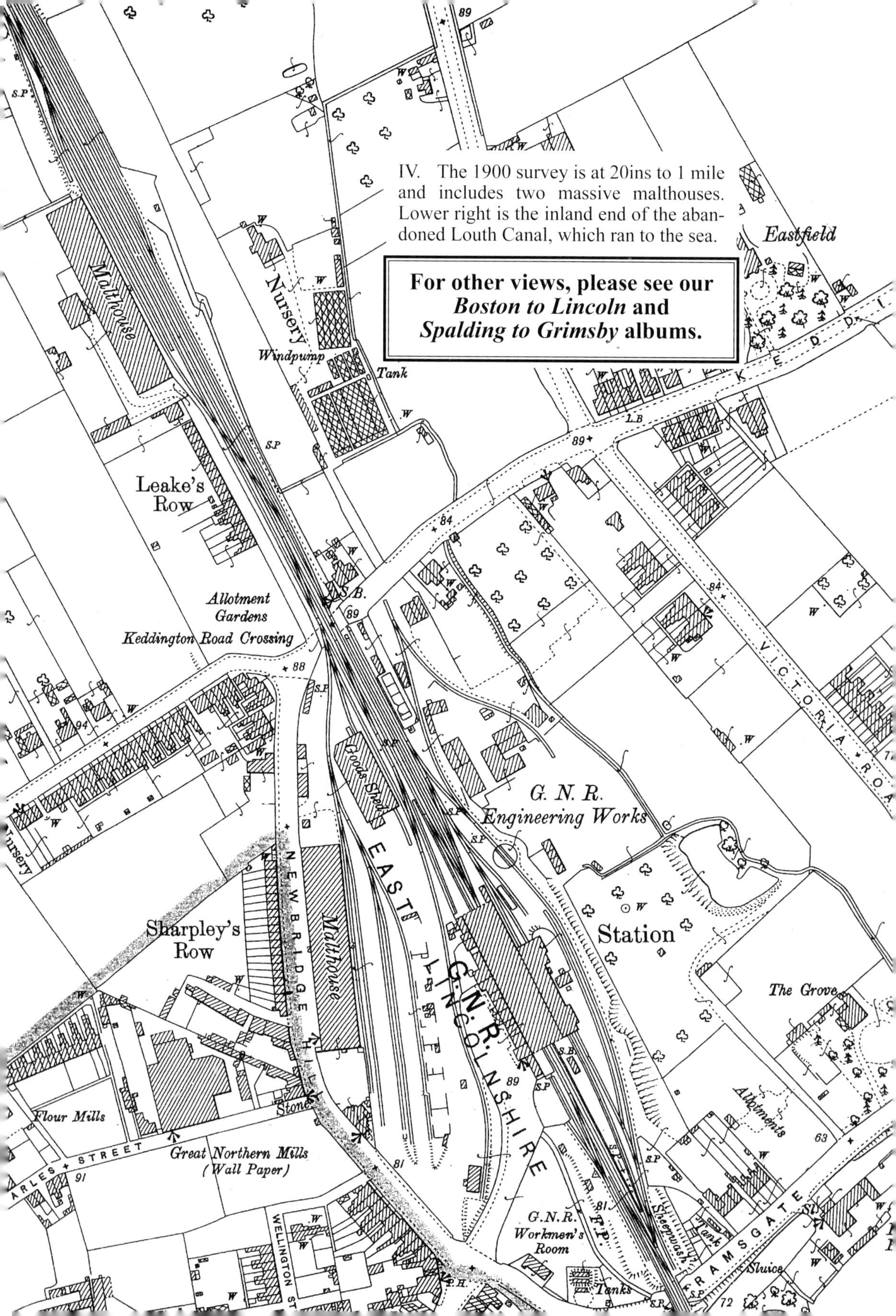

IV. The 1900 survey is at 20ins to 1 mile and includes two massive malthouses. Lower right is the inland end of the abandoned Louth Canal, which ran to the sea.

For other views, please see our *Boston to Lincoln* and *Spalding to Grimsby* albums.

6. We look north from the down platform ramp and find the North Box of 1887. It closed in December 1980 when freight traffic ceased. Seen on 11th September 1968 is the massive goods shed. (HMRS)

7. The all-over roof was demolished in about 1960 and this 1968 view includes evidence to locate the subway. After much neglect, the building was restored to a high standard. (HMRS)

GRIMOLDBY

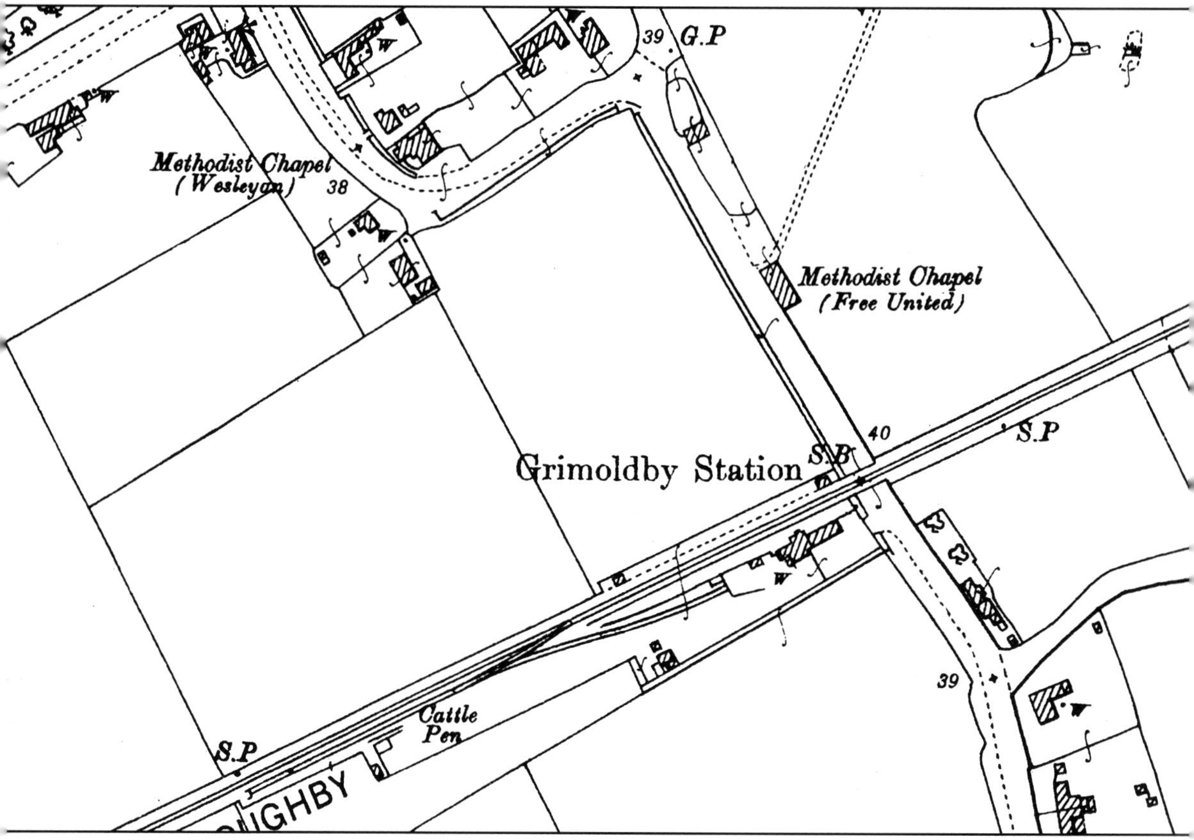

V. The 1906 survey does not include the third Methodist Chapel. The population was around 300 at this time.

8. This card had been postmarked 1907 and unusually features canine caring staff. Of importance are the bidirectional signals and the 1877 signal box, which had 19 levers. (P.Laming coll.)

9. These two photographs are from 1960, this one showing a train bound for Louth behind class B1 4-6-0 no. 61098, a type introduced by the LNER in 1942. (Stations UK)

10. This view is from the signal box shortly before withdrawal of all traffic on 5th December 1960. The goods yard is on the right and the parcels shed is near the main building, which was still standing in 2015. (Stations UK)

SALTFLEETBY

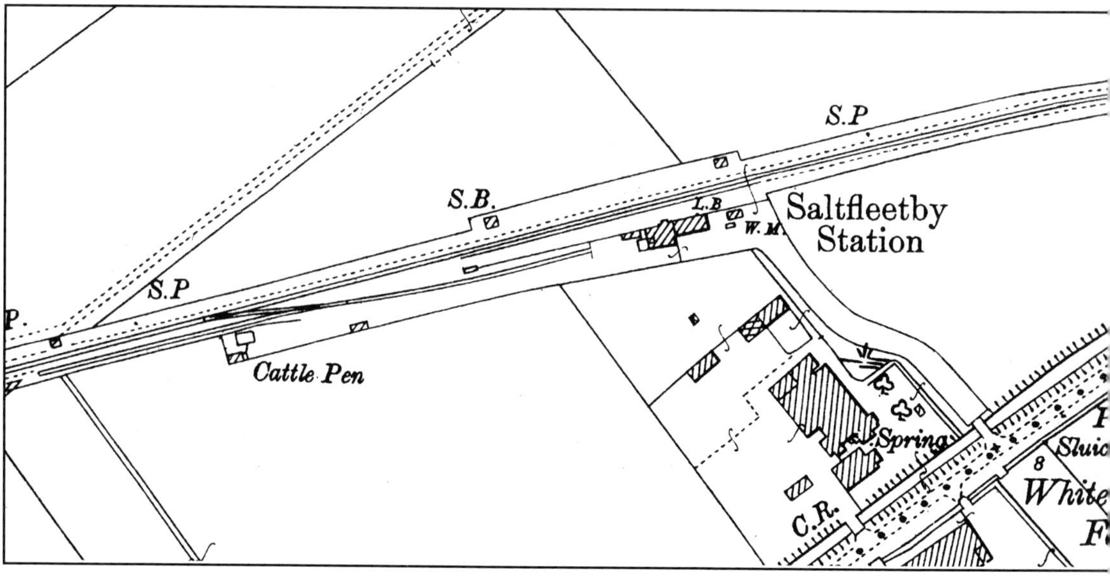

VI. The 1906 map has the beginning of the curve to the coast on the right. The goods yard has a weighing machine (W.M.), but no crane. There were 508 residents in 1901, dropping to 459 in 1961. Many locals say "Solerty".

11. Both photos are from 9th April 1960 and this one is from the signal box, looking over the staff vegetable allotments. The roofless building contained facilities for gentlemen. The white posts on the left carried signal wires. (E.Wilmshurst)

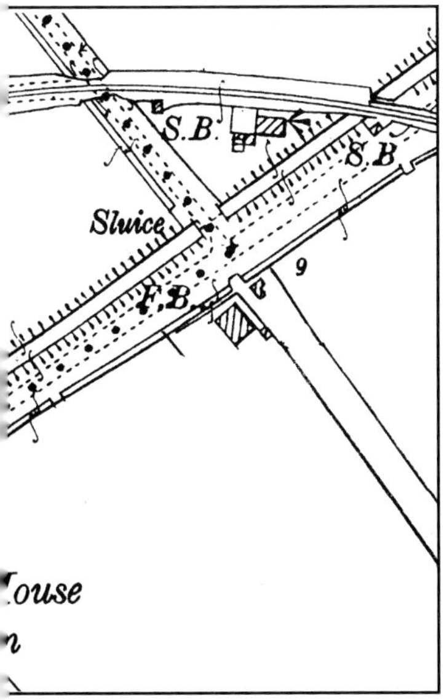

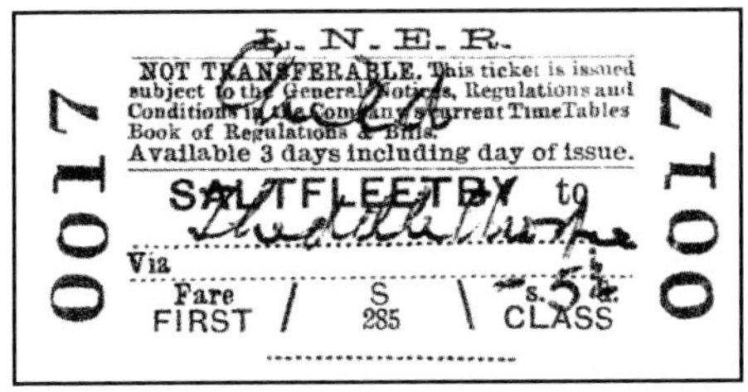

12. The signal box lasted the life of the line and contained 16 levers. All services ceased on 5th December 1960, but the building remained standing. The speed limit sign was for the curve. (E.Wilmshurst)

THEDDLETHORPE

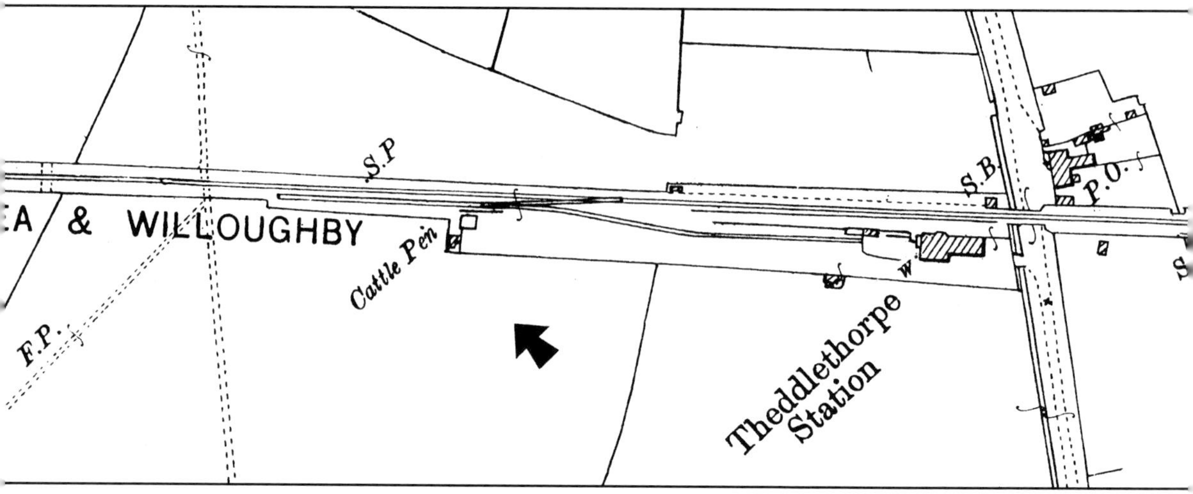

VII. The 1906 survey reveals a familiar story, but with a Post Office nearby.

13. The dates are as for the previous two stations, but the signal box was downgraded to a ground frame in the late 1940s. (LOSA)

14. Sadly, few details have survived of this peaceful location. The entire staff is included, as was customary with early postcards. The population dropped from 780 in 1871 to 491 in 1911. The engine is GNR class F2 0-4-2 no. 951. (P.Laming coll.)

15. A late 1950s southward view includes the parcels shed and better trimmed trees. DMUs were still required to carry oil-lit rear lamps. After closure, the building became a dwelling. (W.A.Camwell/SLS)

16. A clearer record from 9th April 1960 reveals the brick platform edging. The RAF established a bombing and gunnery range nearby during World War II. It closed in 1973; the station had done so on 5th December 1960. (E.Wilmshurst)

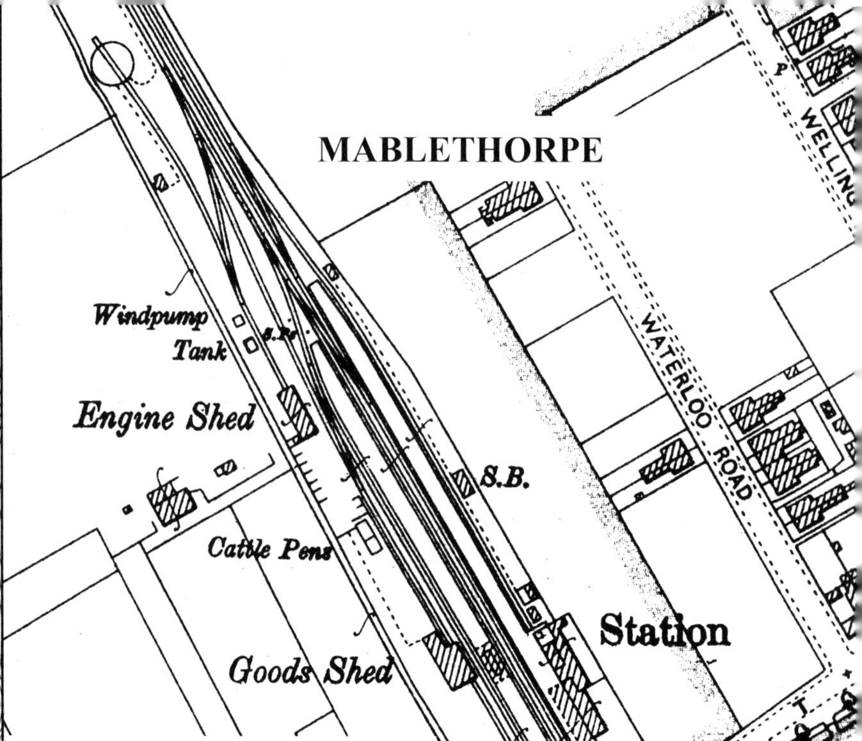

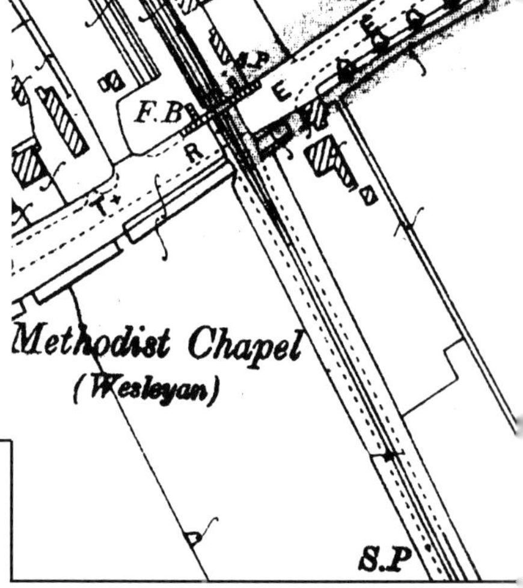

VIII. The main map is from 1906, while inset at 1ins to 1 mile is the 1897 one. This is to show the limited residential development that had taken place; it includes three stations. The main map shows many vacant plots, but the population rose from 640 in 1881, to 934 in 1901 and 5,280 in 1961. A 7¼ins gauge railway for visitors was laid on the seafront at Mablethorpe in the 1930s. The turntable shown was 45ft long and was in use into the 1950s.

17. This view north is from the footbridge by the level crossing, seen in picture 21. The extent of the staff is evident. (P.Laming coll.)

18. A later close-up of them appears to be on some festive occasion. The station was busy enough to justify W.H.Smith running a bookstall at it for many years. Passenger arrivals peaked at 166,000 in 1936. (P.Laming coll.)

19. The engine shed lasted into the 1920s and can just be seen beyond the goods shed, which is on the left. The former closed in 1924. Postmarked 1920, the card footnote stated "Arriving at Mablethorpe"; almost every head is covered. The train had arrived from the south. (P.Laming coll.)

20. We move to the 1950s and class N1 0-6-2T no. 69433 waits on the staff crossing, with one very young admirer watching. A post-war peak of passengers arriving was in 1959, when the figure was 136,400. (W.A.Camwell/SLS)

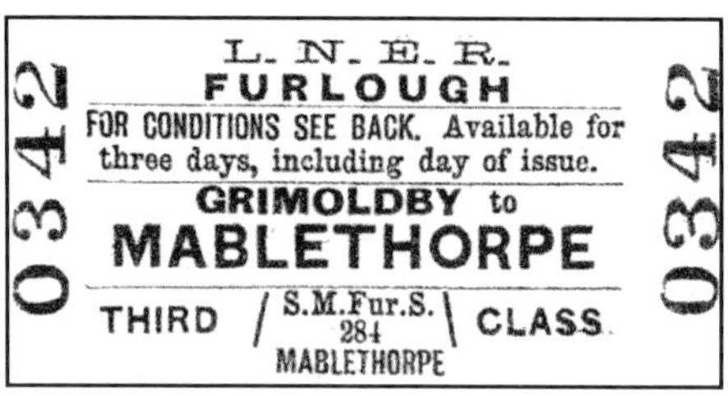

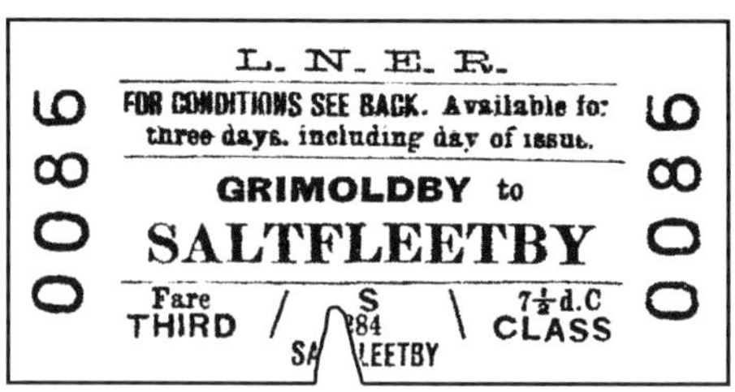

21. Arriving from the south in 1953 is class C12 4-4-2T no. 67379. That was the year of devastating coastal damage and flooding, resulting in 41 deaths and much railway damage. On the right is the lever frame to lock the gates. (Bentley coll.)

22. The downside shelter (left) was completed in 1889 and the footbridge came at about that time. 38,600 people had arrived in 1880, a sign for the future. The water tank on the left had originally been filled by a pump, powered by wind. This is the 1.46pm Louth to Sutton-on-Sea on 13th September 1954, headed by class C12 no. 67398. (R.J.Buckley/SLS)

23. The date is 6th August 1969 and the newsagent's kiosk is still open. The end of the decade as a terminus was nearing, as traffic was diminishing. (J.A.M.Vaughan)

24. Class 4MT 2-6-0 no. 43108 is heading an LCGB railtour on 24th April 1965. From St. Pancras it ran via Leicester, Mansfield, Bardney, Skegness, Boston and back via Corby. There had been a 45ft locomotive turntable here until 1954, when a 52ft one arrived. The signal box had 40 levers and lasted the life of the line. (Colour-Rail.com)

25. The date is 28th March 1970 and we see nos. E56442 and 51284 forming the 13.20 to Boston. On the left is the sign GENTLEMEN and below it are fire buckets. This combination was common practice as the former always had a water supply. A Totem sign from one of the lamp posts sold at auction for £3,000 in 2003. (W.A.Camwell/SLS)

26. This view from 28th March 1970 completes our survey. Only platforms 2 and 3 were in use until the end, as was gas lighting. Closure came on 5th October 1970. Freight traffic had ceased on 30th March 1964. (SLS)

SOUTH OF MABLETHORPE

27. The location is in the centre of the next map; the box is shown on it, but there is no track north of the road, yet. The box had seven levers and was in use from 1888 until October 1970. The picture is from that year, showing that its name was never changed. (J.A.Evans/HMRS)

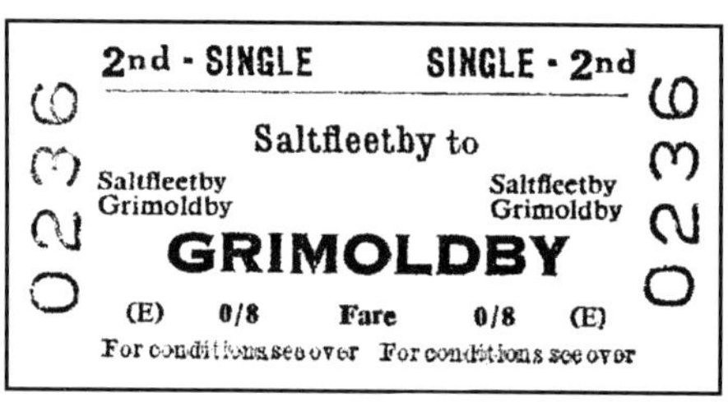

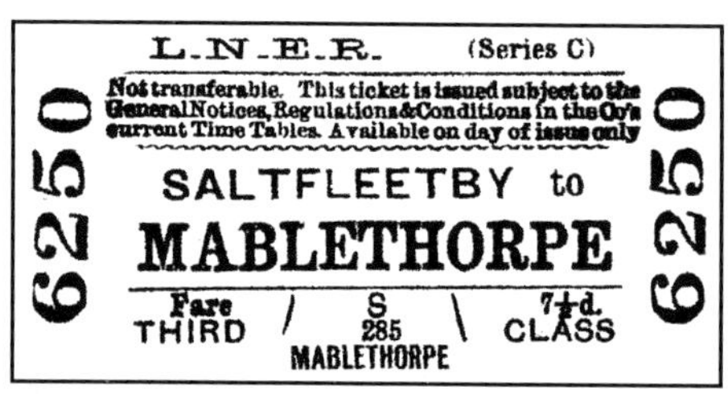

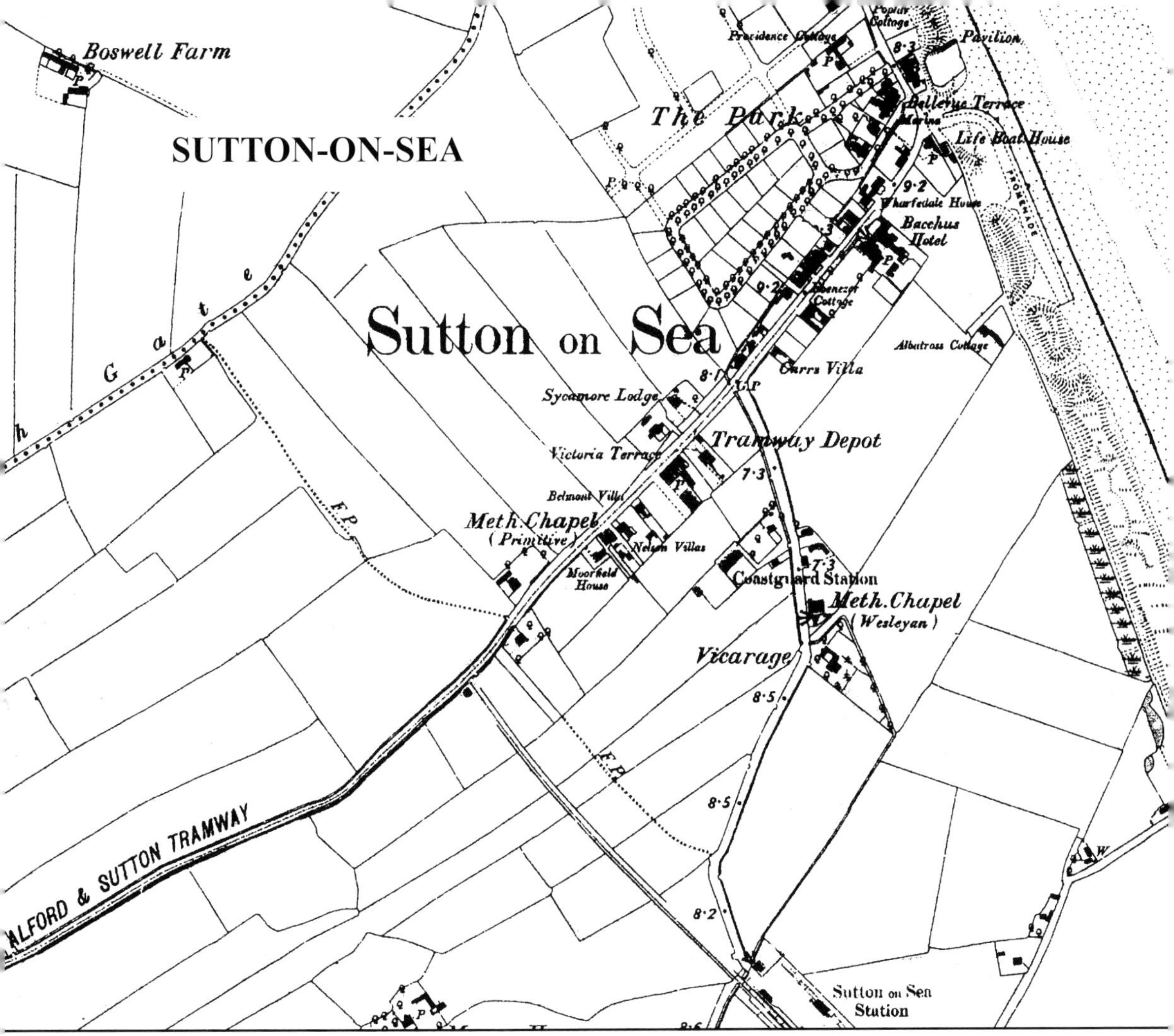

IX. The Alford & Sutton Tramway of 1884-89 is shown faintly on this 1888 survey, enlarged to 8ins to 1 mile. Its terminus is close to the Bacchus Hotel. Its depot is above both Methodist Chapels. It is illustrated in picture 65 at Alford, in our *Spalding to Grimsby* album.

28. The A&ST opening day on 2nd April 1884 was recorded badly near the town centre. The track was 2ft 6ins gauge. The tram engine had a steel skirt around its wheels and a vertical boiler. The passenger car was usually behind the wagons. (A.Dudman coll.)

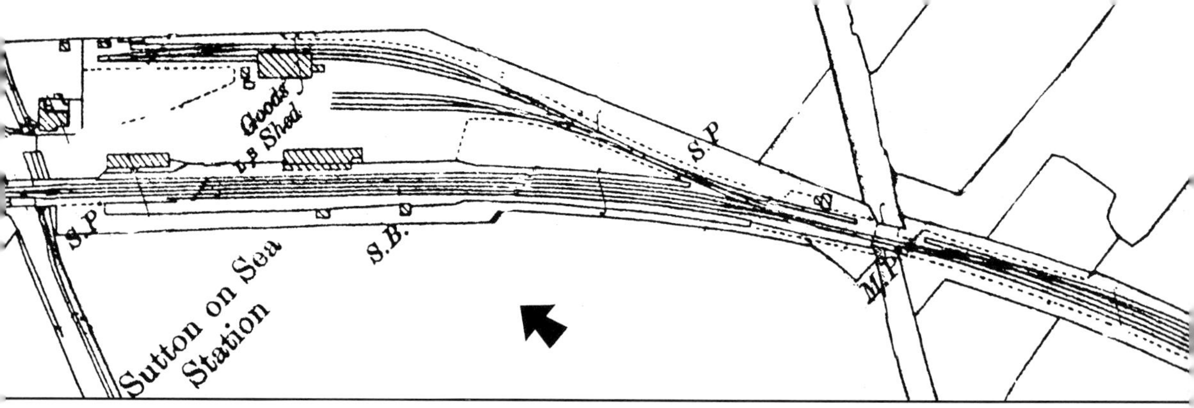

X. The 1905 survey indicates that the up platform had a letter box.

29. Overlapping crossing gates were an unusual subject for a postcard. The gate man is profiled and transport for the wealthy is emphasised. (P.Laming coll.)

30. Passengers arriving here in 1888 numbered 38,600, but there were only 362 residents and 835 in 1911. Left is the signal box which had 16 levers and was worked for the life of the line. The boards of the staff crossing formed the rodding tunnel. Sutton-in-the-Marsh was the name used until the railway arrived. (LOSA)

31. Seen from a train bound for Louth on 30th August 1956 is evidence that the signalman had the joys of a garden and a stove. Unusually, the glazing was limited. (H.C.Casserley)

32. By 1961, the population had risen to 1,341 and diesel units had arrived. Ten years later the site was cleared to make room for more houses, but the main building was saved, albeit short term. Goods traffic ceased on 30th March 1964. (W.A.Camwell/SLS)

MUMBY ROAD

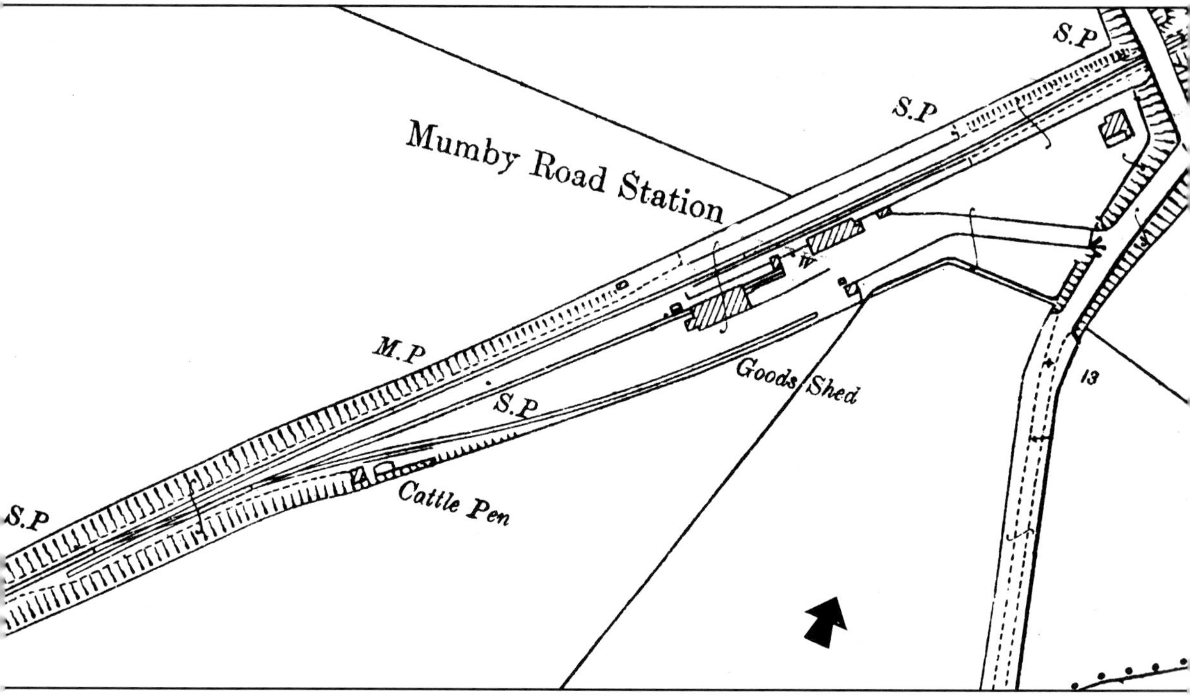

XI. The 1906 issue includes a well close to the station, as there was no mains water. The goods shed housed a 30cwt crane and the yard lasted until 30th March 1964. The up platform is shown: a loop line was eventually provided.

33. A 1938 view features class C12 4-4-2T no. 4539. This type was common here from 1921. The map shows two platforms, but only one track. The out of use loop was reinstated on 27th May 1936. The main building remained after closure. (LOSA)

34. Bidirectional signalling on one track is evident although the signal box is not. Grain drying is in progress. Blowing off is class J11 0-6-0 no. 64320, heading the 10.42am Louth to Firsby on 14th September 1954. (R.J.Buckley/SLS)

35. This southward panorama is from 1958 and shows more wagons than would be needed to supply coal to Mumby, a village of around 200 souls. Maybe they were collecting potatoes or other root crops. (Stations UK)

36. Included in this view from the rear of a DMU on 9th April 1960 is the small signal box. It had 14 levers and closed early, on 17th July 1965. A trolley track is in the foreground. (E.Wilmshurst)

37. This sad and forlorn sight was taken at the dilapidated and neglected station on 9th August 1969. Some trains only stopped by request and amazing to relate that this train stopped not by the request of an alighting or boarding passenger, but by the photographer, who was already travelling on the train and was desperate for a picture at the location! The station gained fame in Flanders & Swann's song, *The Slow Train*. (J.A.M.Vaughan)

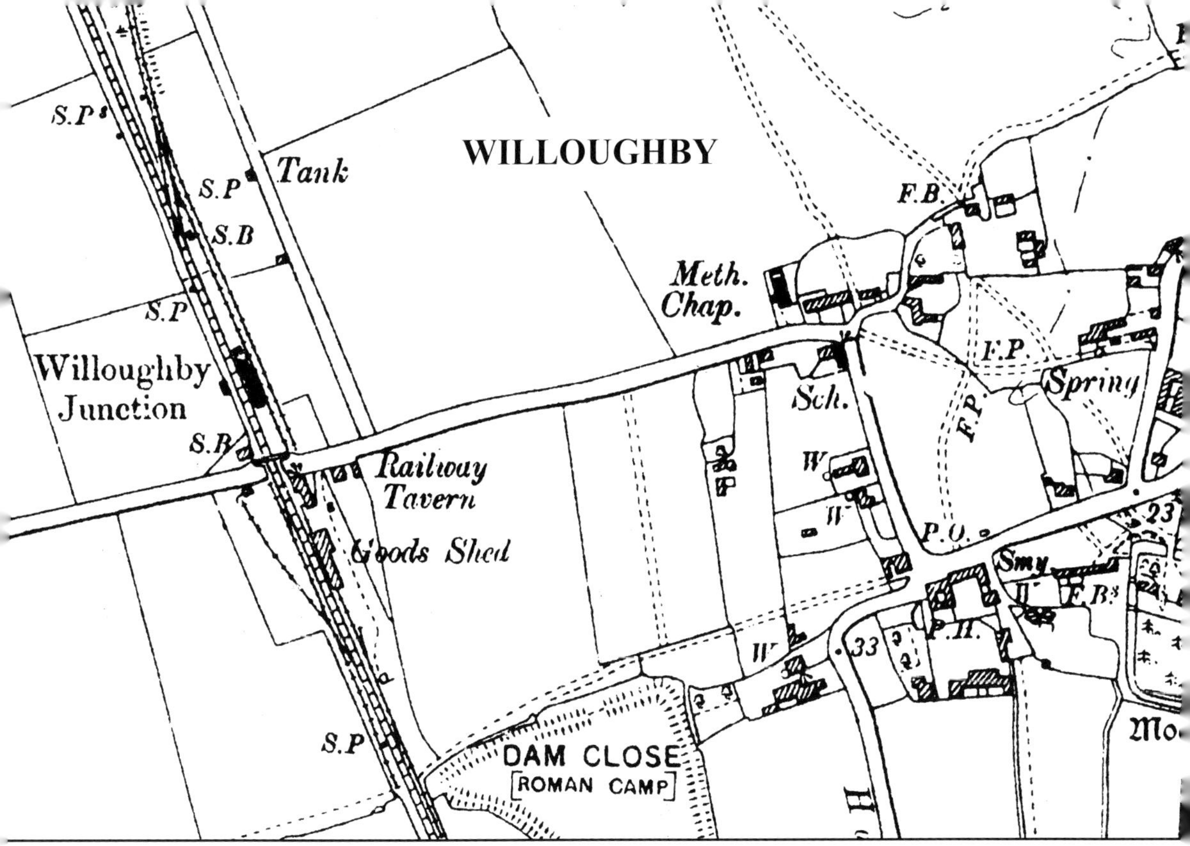

XII. The 1905 map at 12ins to 1 mile reveals the relationship of the station to the community. Smy refers to the smithy, which was essential to pre-railway travellers for horseshoes and wheel repairs.

38. A late Victorian view northwards shows the second station. The first had been behind the camera and was in use from 1848 until 1886, when the Loop was completed and the junction came into use. (P.Laming coll.)

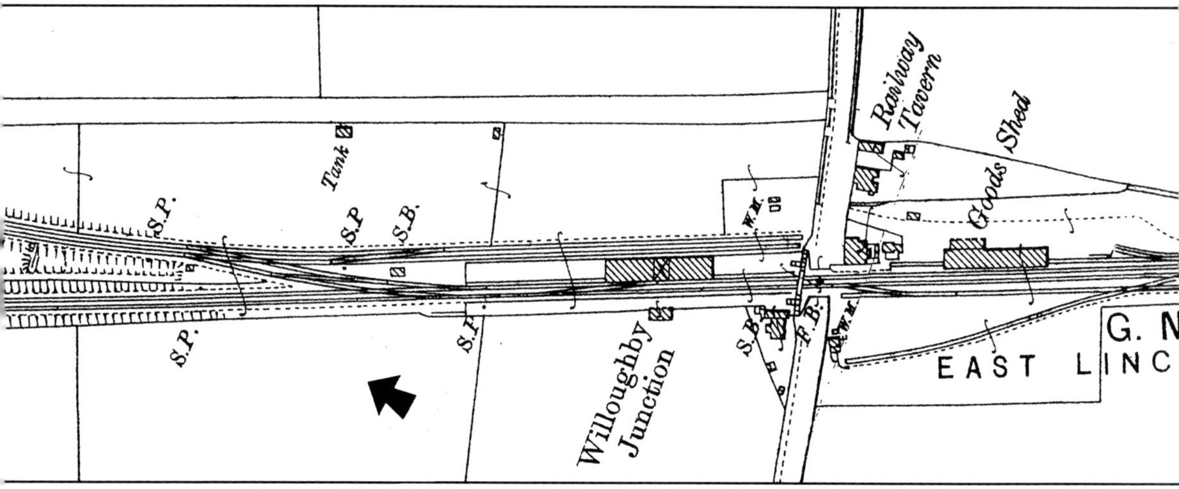

XIII. The same edition, but at 30ins to 1 mile, gives more detail, such as the weighing machine (W.M.) for road vehicles.

39. Two panoramas from the footbridge appeared on postcards. The milk churn indicates another commodity conveyed by passenger trains in large quantities. (P.Laming coll.)

40. Fine topiary would have enhanced the holiday ambience for those visitors changing trains here. The locomotive water tank was distant from the track, probably to minimise well depth. (P.Laming coll.)

Other views can be found in pictures 59 to 64 in our *Spalding to Grimsby* album.

41. Arriving with the 9.49am from Louth is class C12 4-4-2T no. 67384 on 14th September 1954. It was ex-GNR. The crossover to release the engine is shown in picture 48. (R.J.Buckley/SLS)

42. Two views from 11th July 1959 reveal a high standard of maintenance and mostly modern flat-bottomed rail. Point rodding runs to the crossover and the junction points. (J.M.Chesney)

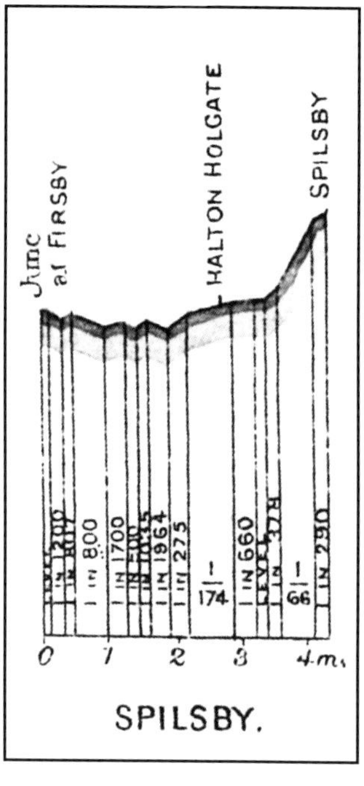

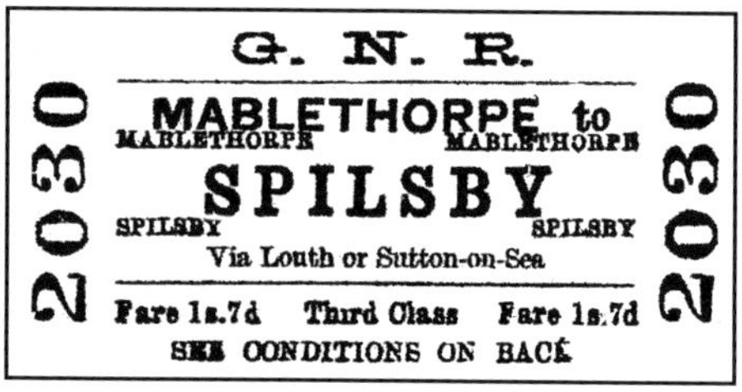

43. A train from Mablethorpe runs onto the up line, hauled by class B1 4-6-0 no. 61209. There were through trains from the Loop to Derby, Manchester and Nottingham at this period, but mainly at peak times. (J.M.Chesney)

44. The signal box had 50 levers and functioned during the life of the Loop. Many of its smaller stations and boxes required a fresh water supply, hence the cans in the foreground. It is seen in its final year. (Colour-Rail.com)

45. Junction Box had a 20-lever frame and had the same life as the Station Box. It was only manned at busy times. The bay and run-round points were worked from this points cabin, by the station foreman or a senior porter. (E.Wilmshurst)

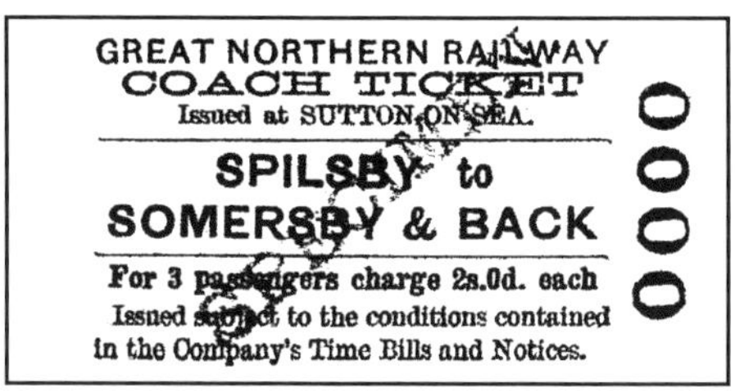

46. The up starting signal is off ready for a Boston-bound DMU to depart. The other one will probably wait for a down train and a small crowd to use the footbridge. (W.A.Camwell/SLS)

47. A northward view from 7th April 1967 includes the house for the station master, which was part of the original station. The sidings on the left were likewise; the goods shed was built on the site of the first up platform. Freight traffic ceased on 20th May 1966. (Milepost 92½)

48. The south end of the bay is seen on the same day. All was eventually demolished, except for the house. A rail mounted gun had been kept in the sidings here during part of World War I. (Milepost 92½)

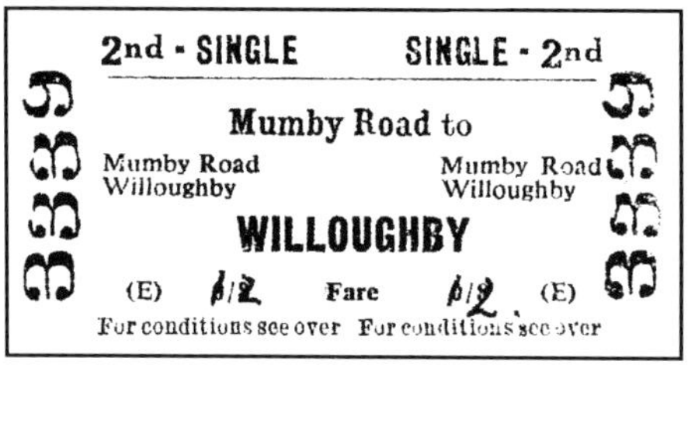

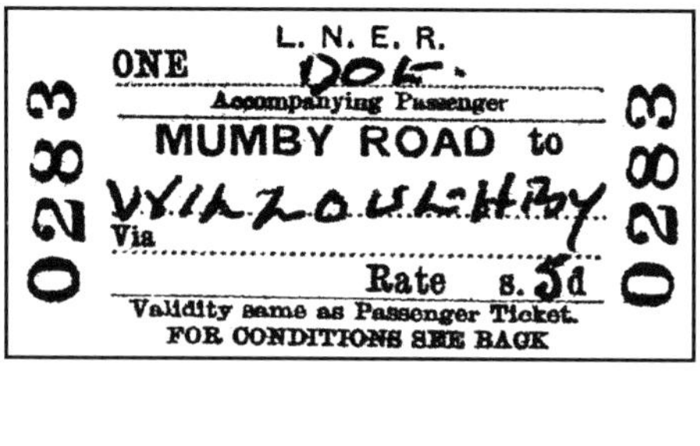

2. Spilsby Branch

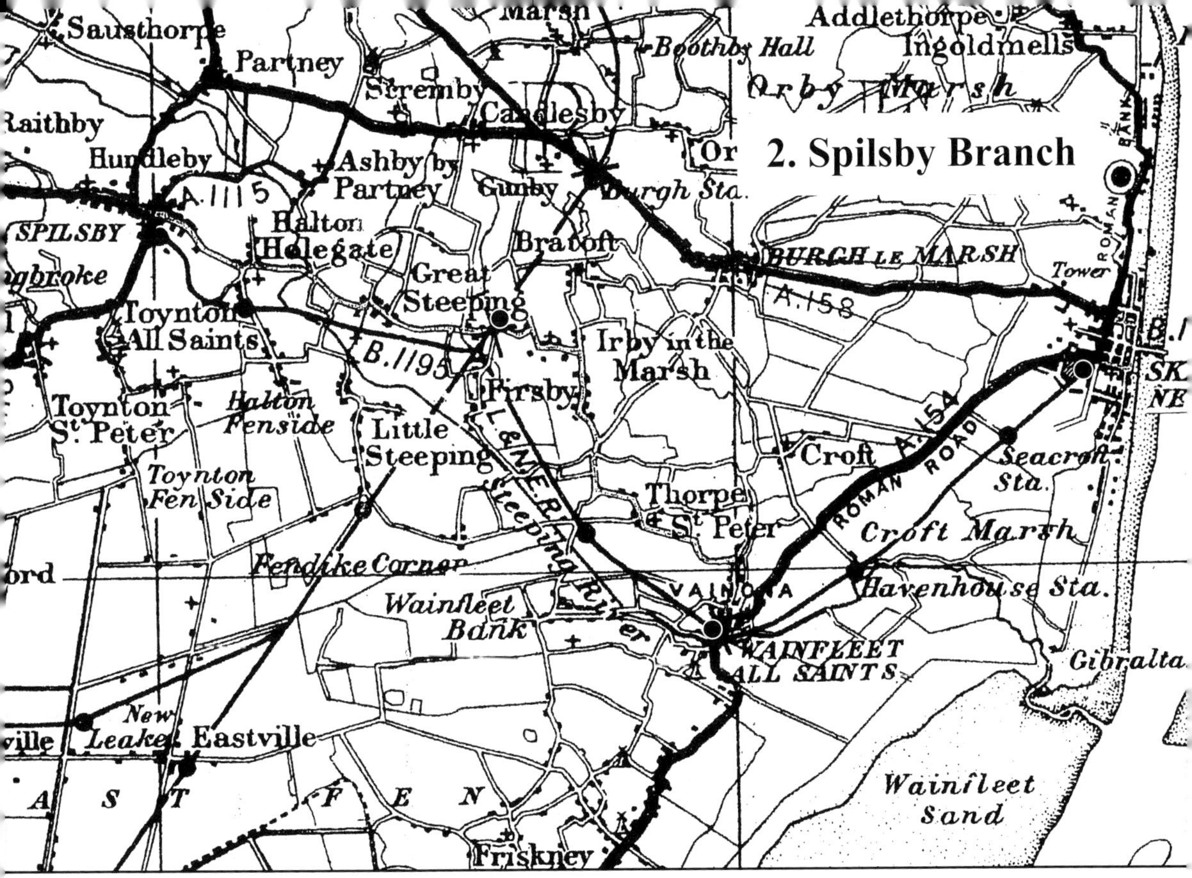

XIV. The 1946 edition at ¼ins to 1 mile has Firsby station below the 'n' of Great Steeping, near the centre of the extract. The branch to Spilsby runs uphill to the left, whilst the almost level line to Skegness terminates on the right. Gibraltar became a nature reserve.

FIRSBY

49. Crowds from down trains arriving on the left platform and bound for Skegness had to use the bridge, which was always devoid of a roof. At peak times, when most were carrying suitcases, the branch train departure would be changed to platform 1. North Points Box is in the distance. (Stations UK)

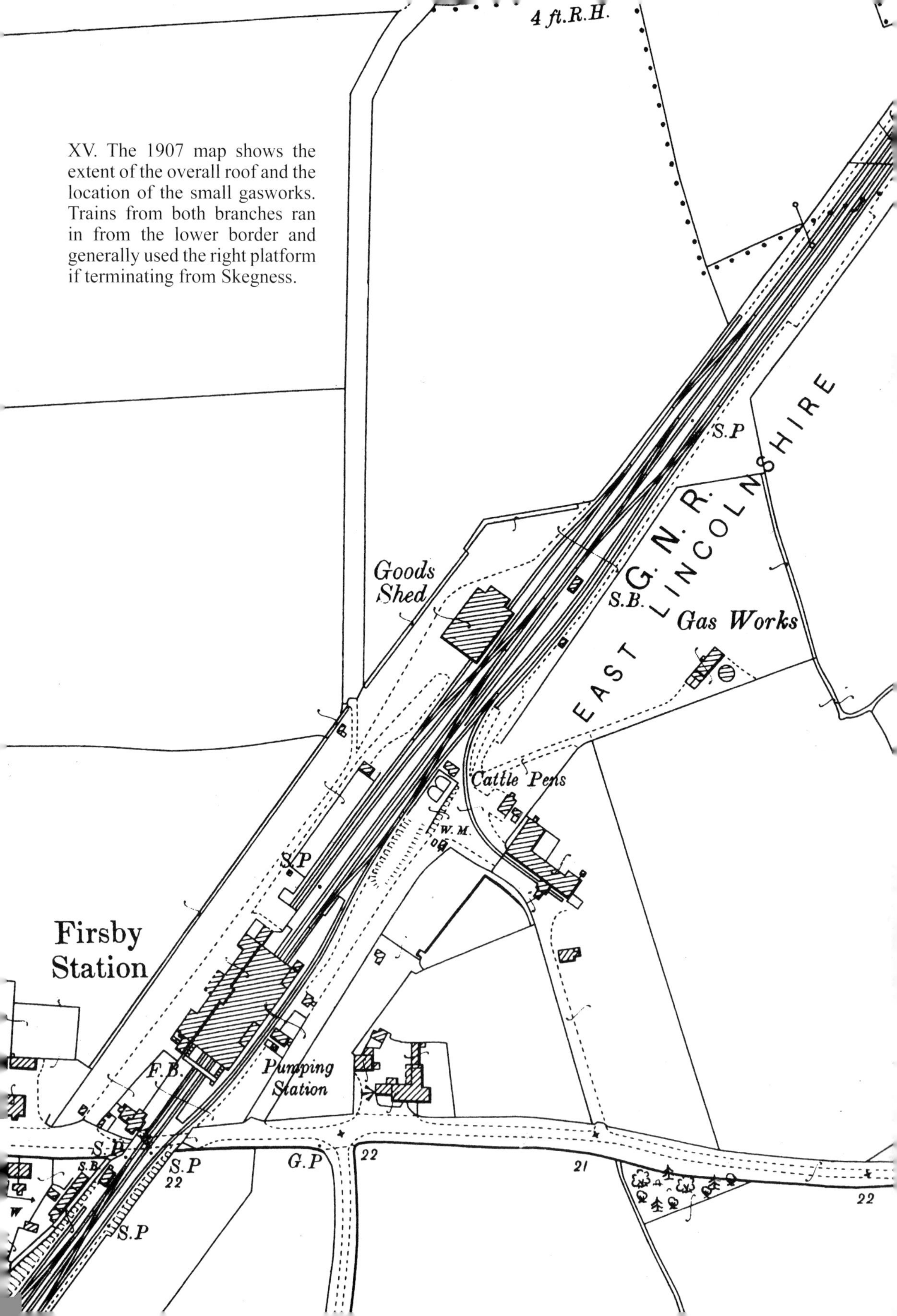

XV. The 1907 map shows the extent of the overall roof and the location of the small gasworks. Trains from both branches ran in from the lower border and generally used the right platform if terminating from Skegness.

50. This was the prospective passengers' perspective and few would know that behind the nearest wall was the domestic backyard. Austin Sevens were produced from 1922 to 1939, so the picture cannot be dated easily. (Colour-Rail.com)

51. The RCTS "Lincolnshire Railtour" is seen on 16th May 1954, after traversing the Spilsby branch. The train locomotive, ex-GNR class J6 0-6-0 no. 64199, has just taken water. RAF Spilsby was north of here and generated extra traffic between 1943 and 1958. (N.W.Sprinks)

SOUTH OF FIRSBY

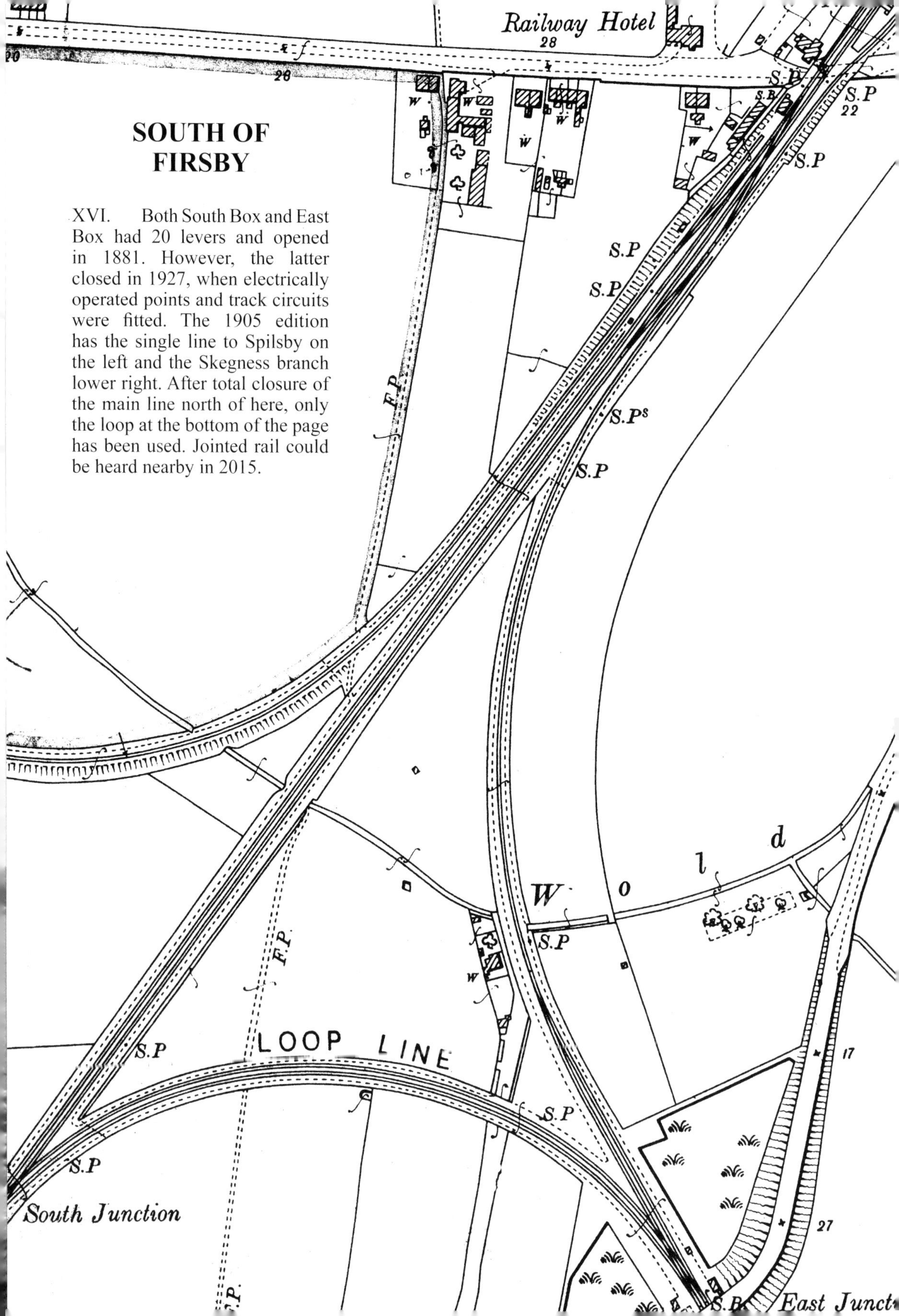

XVI. Both South Box and East Box had 20 levers and opened in 1881. However, the latter closed in 1927, when electrically operated points and track circuits were fitted. The 1905 edition has the single line to Spilsby on the left and the Skegness branch lower right. After total closure of the main line north of here, only the loop at the bottom of the page has been used. Jointed rail could be heard nearby in 2015.

56. Southwest of Firsby there was a triangular junction with only a single line connecting Firsby with the direct double track line from Boston to Skegness. The whole of the south Lincolnshire area was rich with somersault signalling, as seen above this Skegness bound DMU on 20th April 1970. Firsby station can be seen in the background. (J.A.M.Vaughan)

HALTON HOLGATE

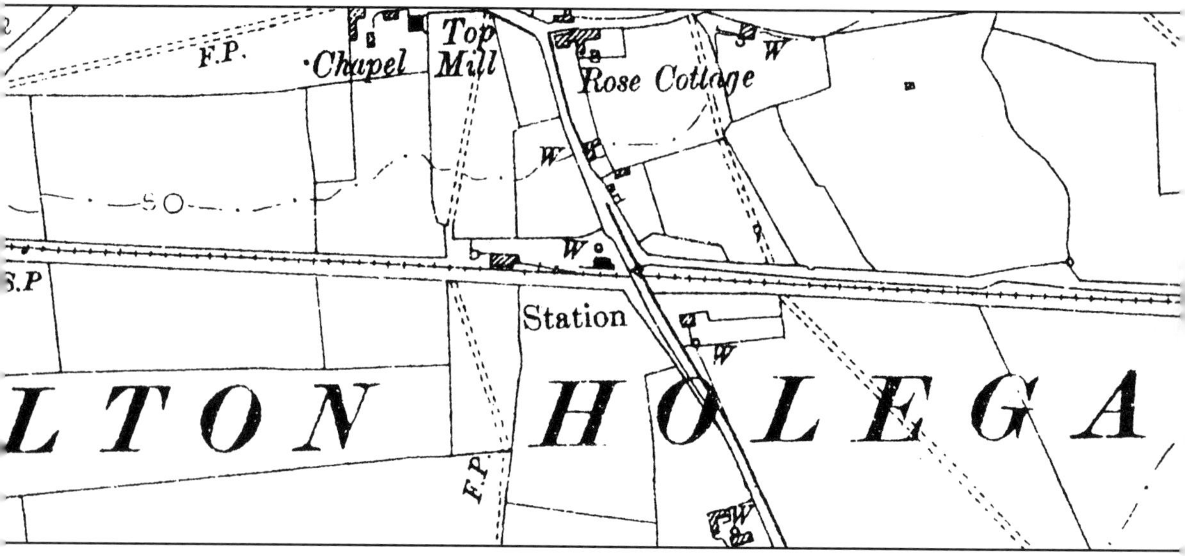

XVII. The 1906 map at 12ins to 1 mile fails to show that the siding through the goods shed connected to the running line at the west end. The village had 406 residents in 1901 and its fringe is on the map.

57. The fine building stands today as a residence, albeit with a conservatory across the platforms, where the canopy survived into the early 1950s. The photo is from 1953. The goods shed contained a 25cwt crane. (Stations UK)

58. While the branch closed to passengers in 1939, freight continued until 1st December 1958. Fruit and flowers were notable loads from here to London, transfer to expresses being needed at Firsby. (W.A.Camwell/SLS)

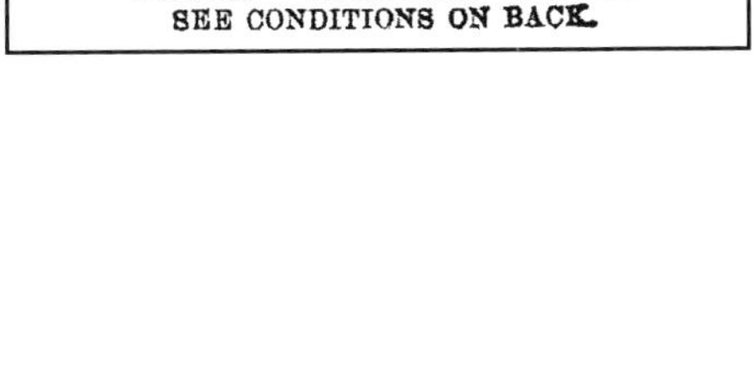

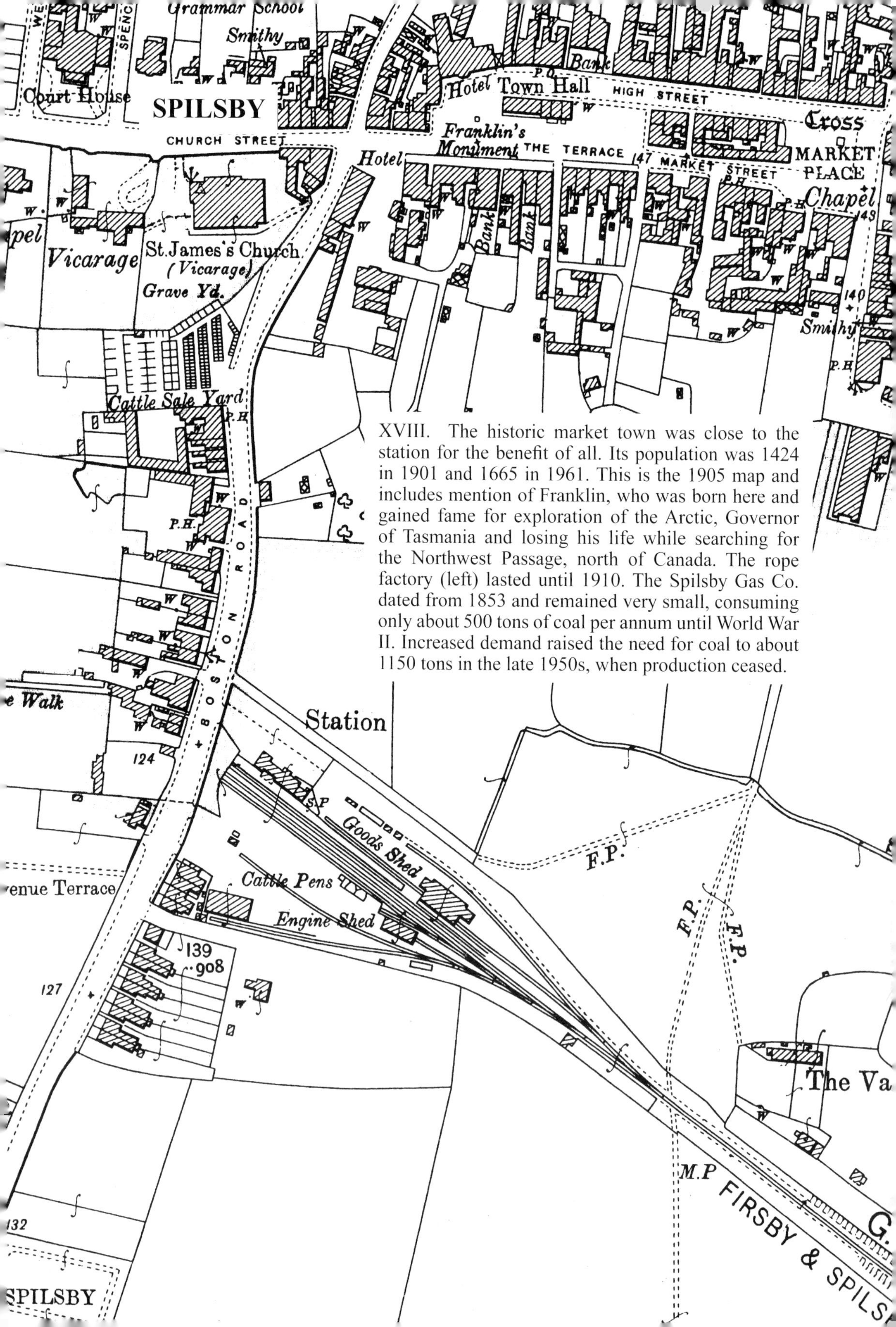

XVIII. The historic market town was close to the station for the benefit of all. Its population was 1424 in 1901 and 1665 in 1961. This is the 1905 map and includes mention of Franklin, who was born here and gained fame for exploration of the Arctic, Governor of Tasmania and losing his life while searching for the Northwest Passage, north of Canada. The rope factory (left) lasted until 1910. The Spilsby Gas Co. dated from 1853 and remained very small, consuming only about 500 tons of coal per annum until World War II. Increased demand raised the need for coal to about 1150 tons in the late 1950s, when production ceased.

59. An early postcard reveals a 2-2-2 with a train of four-wheelers, plus the shunting horse. The crane was later listed as having a 5-ton capacity. (P.Laming coll.)

60. A later card has the main gate in line with the chimney of the weigh bridge office and St. James's Church tower. The coal stack would be for station use. (P.Laming coll.)

61. The final card has the usual display of posed people and prolific promotions. One reveals that the GNR was still operating the trains. There was no signal box, as the "One Engine in Steam" rule was applied to the branch. (P.Laming coll.)

62. The engine shed is on the left in this 1950 photo, but it would soon be demolished. It had housed a single tank engine until 1939. Water was raised from a well, using a steam injector coupled by a hose to the locomotive's train heating pipe. A fresh engine came every week from Boston shed. (R.M.Casserley coll.)

63. The brake van hides two levers, which worked the points under the adjacent tank wagon. Cattle wagons are on the right in this 1953 view. The staff had numbered eight in the early years. (Stations UK)

64. The RCTS "Lincolnshire Railtour" of 16th May 1964 also visited Horncastle and the Mablethorpe Loop. We have already seen it in picture 51. The main buildings were demolished in 1965, but the goods shed was retained for fresh purposes. (N.W.Sprinks)

3. Coningsby Loop

CONINGSBY

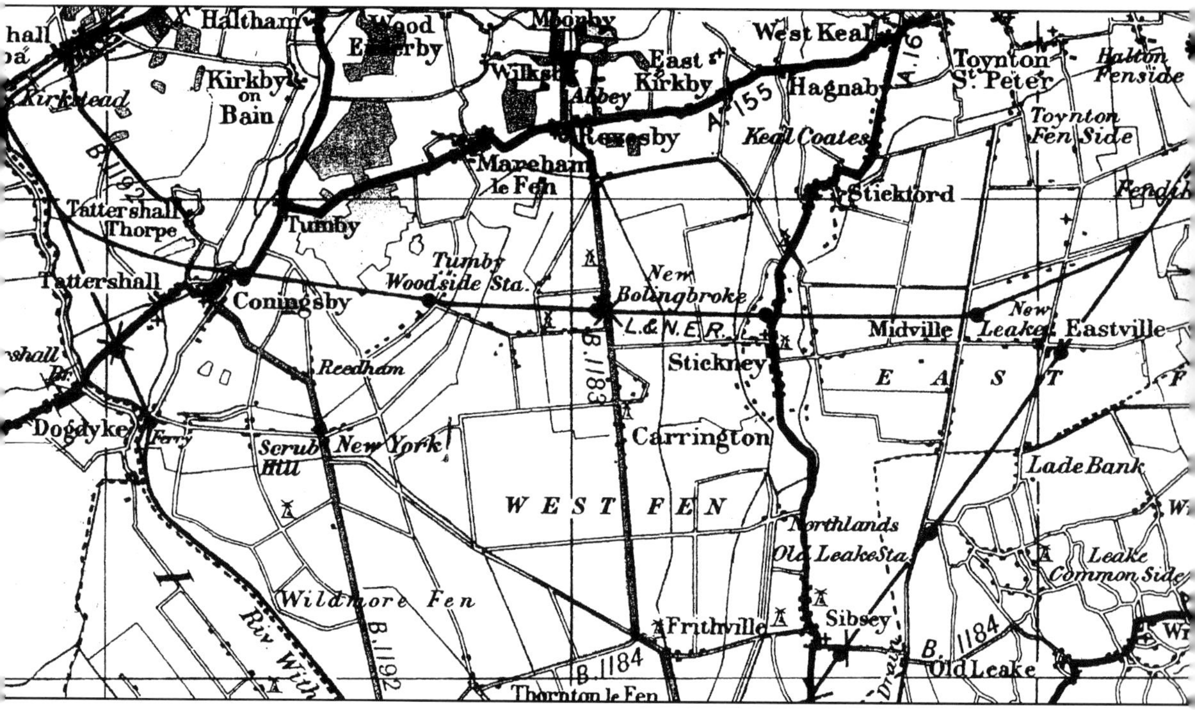

XIXa. Scaled at ¼ins to 1 mile, the 1946 edition shows the 1913 link between the Boston to Lincoln line (left) and the Boston to Louth route (right). The link was officially named the Kirkstead and Little Steeping Railway, but was known locally as "The New Line". It opened as a Light Railway with a 25mph speed restriction imposed by the Board of Trade; this was later increased to 50mph. Although laid as a double track, one line was lifted in 1916 to provide materials for use in France during World War I. Unfortunately, the plan was thwarted as the vessel carrying the material was sunk in the English Channel. The second track was reinstated in 1923. Since 1916, there had been just two stopping trains, weekdays only.

65. A westward view in 1939 includes an ex-GNR somersault signal in the off position. The map shows that the line passes over two waterways in the distance. The site was developed for housing after closure in 1970. (Stations UK)

66. Looking eastwards in 1961, we see a van in the single siding and also the signal box, which had 25 levers and was in use until 29th January 1969. One train terminated here daily from the mid-1940s for 20 years. It left Lincoln at about 10.30pm and carried mainly revelling servicemen. All licensed premises closed at that time by law. (Stations UK)

XIXb. The 1951 edition includes the northern part of the village. It had 1087 residents in 1901 and 2629 in 1961. The maps in this section are at about 10ins to 1 mile; none at 25ins were produced. The goods yard closed on 30th March 1964. RAF Coningsby was established south of the village in 1941 and it became the home of the Battle of Britain Memorial Flight in 1957.

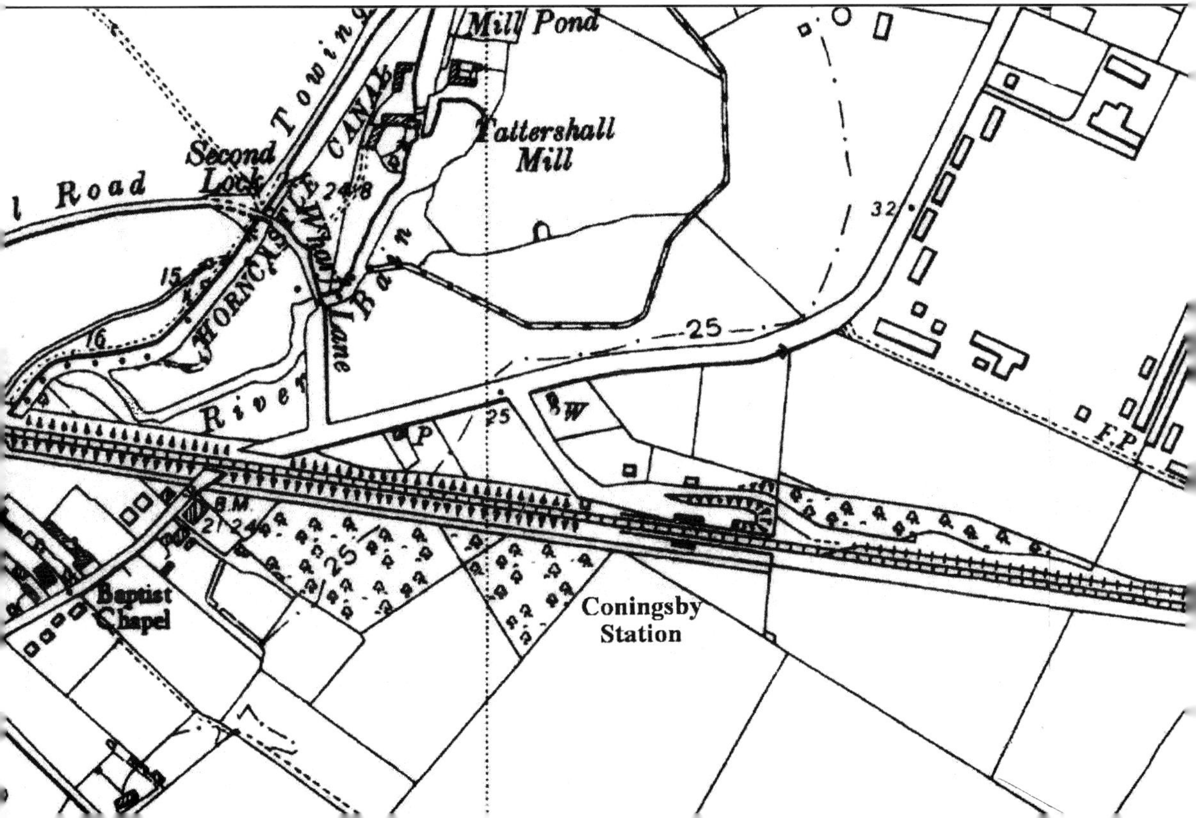

TUMBY WOODSIDE

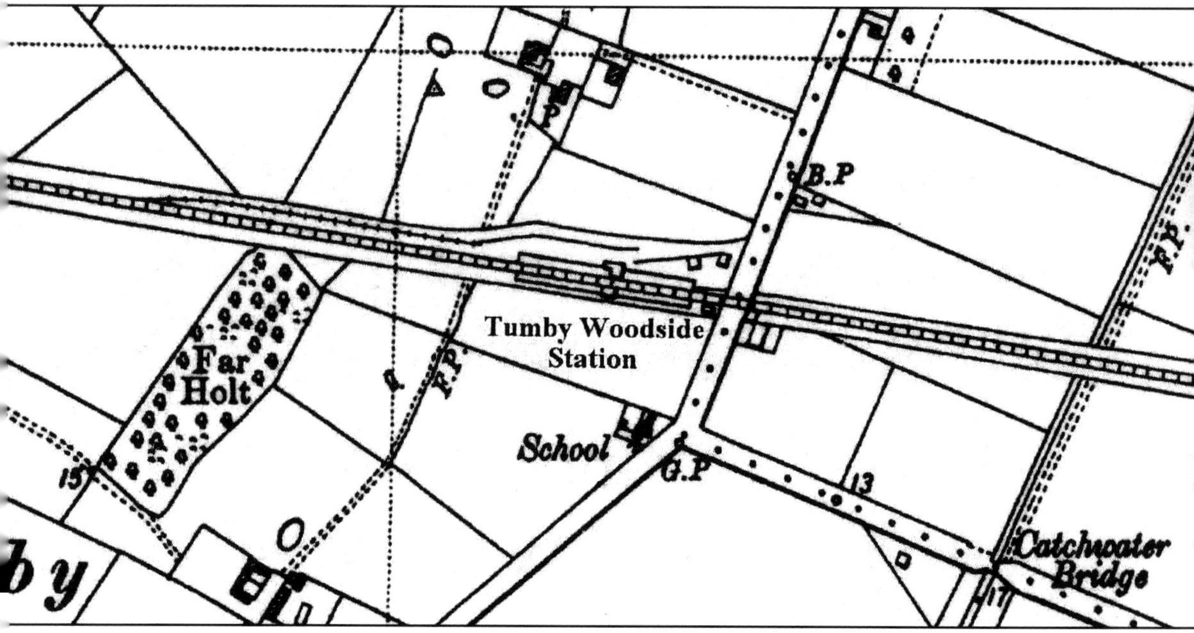

XX. The small hamlet is three miles from the village of Tumby. This is the 1951 issue. Like Mumby Road and Dogdyke, the station was immortalised in the Flanders and Swann song *The Slow Train*.

67. The new station was photographed soon after its opening in 1913. A population of 309 had been recorded in 1901. The signal box had 25 levers and was used until line closure. (P.Laming coll.)

68. A panorama from about 1939 includes the siding, noted for its potato traffic. There were also splendid floral displays. By 1948, three trains called each way, but one to Woodhall Junction only called upon request. There were no Sunday trains. (Stations UK)

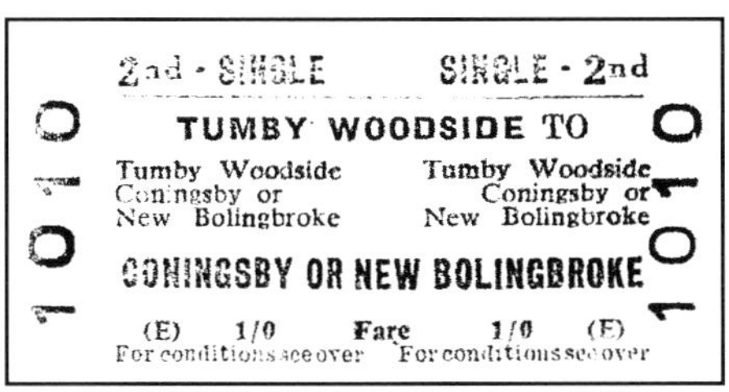

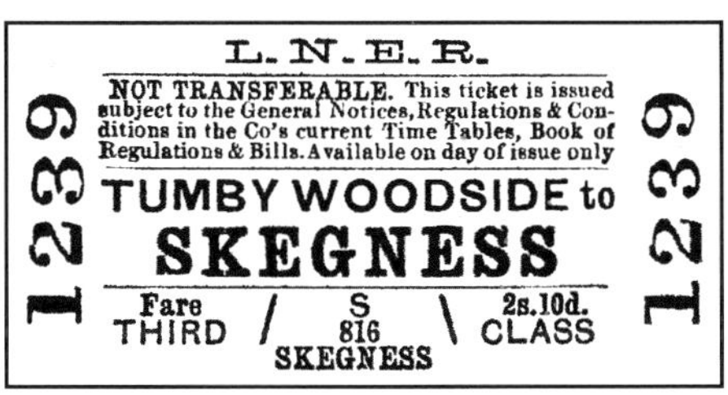

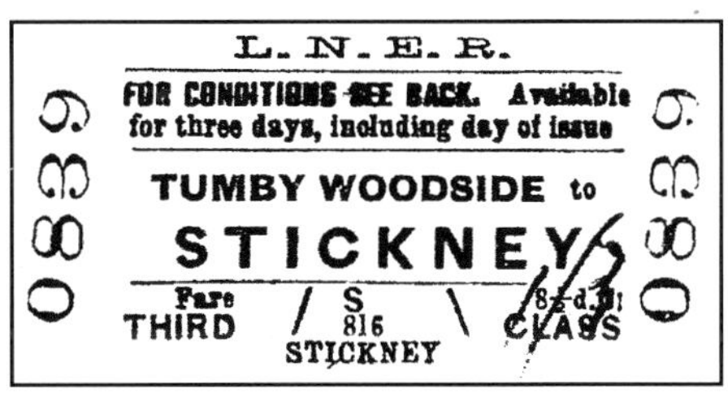

NEW BOLINGBROKE

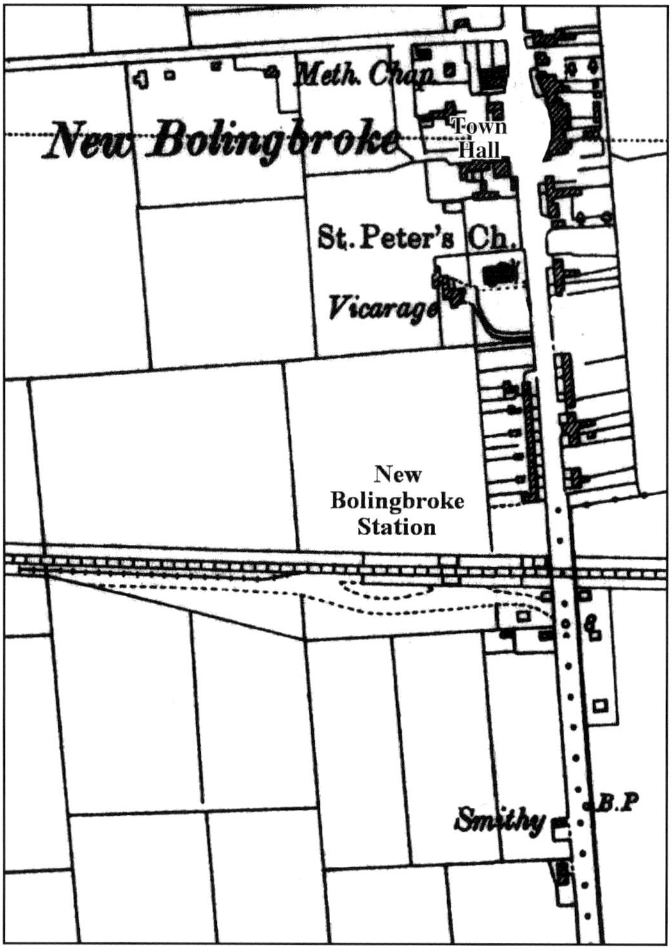

XXI.The 1951 edition includes the town hall and the third siding on the loop. The church yard was less than 8ft above sea level.

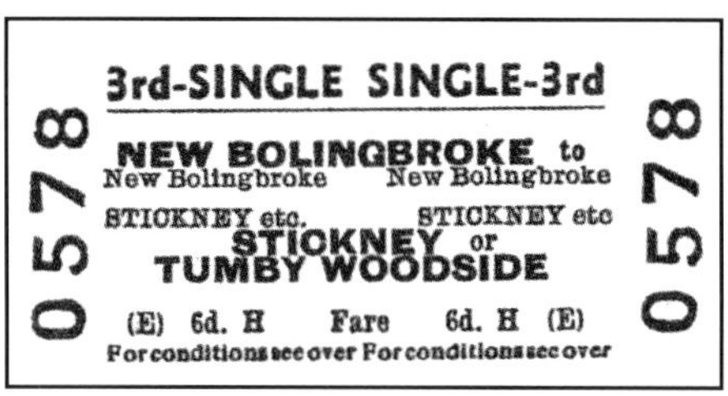

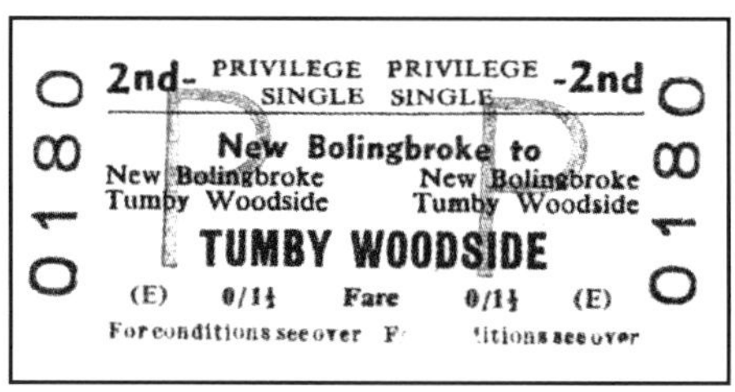

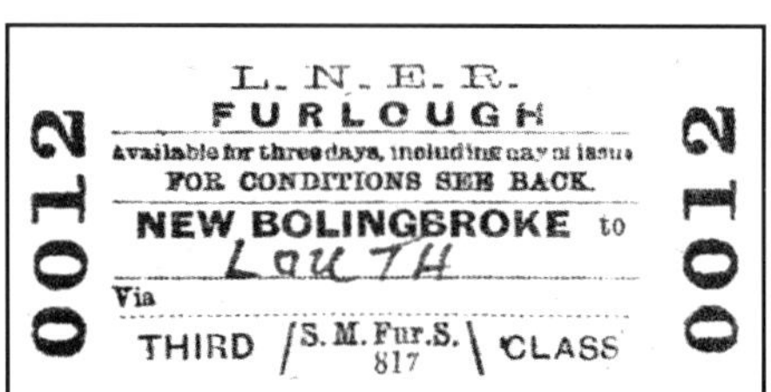

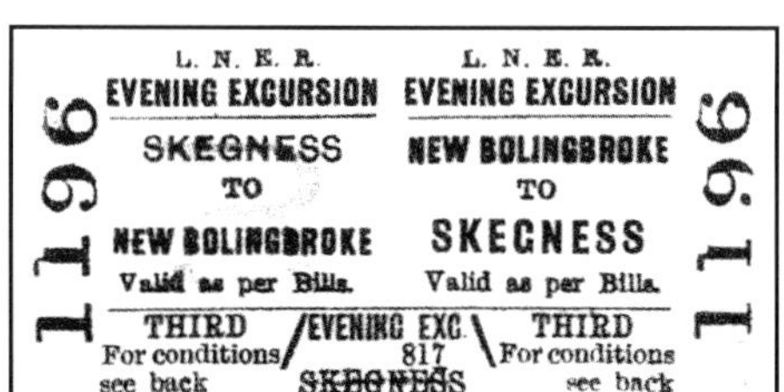

69. Level crossing regulations were different on Light Railways, as can be seen in this early postcard view, during shunting. The box had a 30-lever frame and closed with the line. (P.Laming coll.)

70. Another floral treat was to be seen here in about 1939. In the distance is the goods yard, which was open until 30th March 1964, as were the others on the Loop. (Stations UK)

74. An eastward view reveals standard styling. Staffing ceased on 7th October 1968, but trains called until the end. The house was retained, but otherwise the site was levelled. (P.Laming coll.)

75. Two views from September 1969 complete the story, albeit a sad one. Only one seat and one bucket are left. No longer was ash on the track a problem. (HMRS)

76. The glass is almost intact, but all the rodding and wires have been removed. Jointed track prevailed to the end, as did oil lamps. (HMRS)

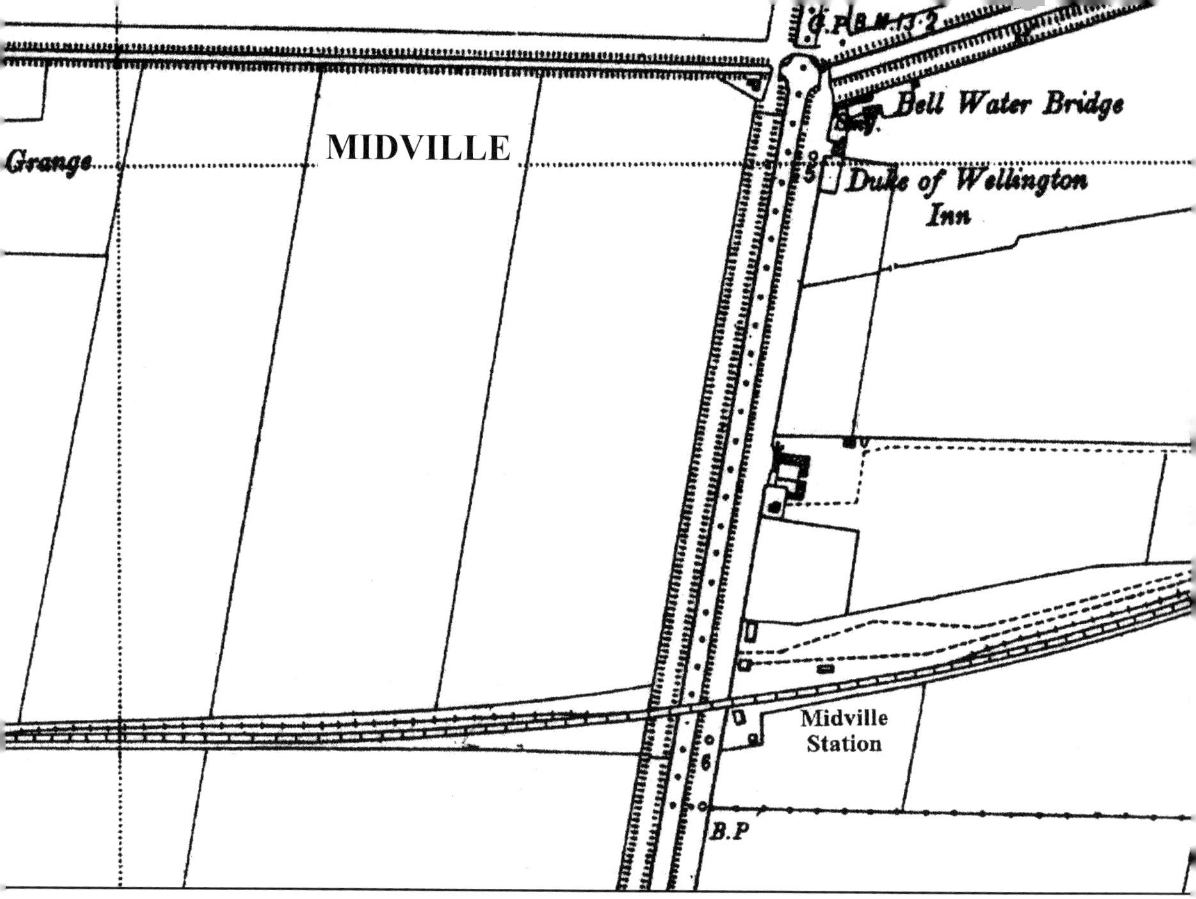

XXIII. The station was north of the village, which housed 205 in 1911 and 244 in 1961. Alongside the road is Hobhole Drain, which is near the centre of East Fen.

77. An eastward view from around 1939 has the loading gauge, although indistinct, and details of the wooden platforms. Timber was used, due to the softness of fenland. The goods siding was not used after 30th March 1964. (Stations UK)

78. This 1950 picture includes part of the points into the refuge siding. Pullman cars were stored in it during World War II. The 30-lever signal box lasted until the end of traffic in 1970. The structures were removed, except the main building on the left. (Stations UK)

79. The station lost its staff on 7th October 1968 and this DMU is seen on 11th July 1969 working the 16.45 from Skegness. There was a train from Mablethorpe and two from Firsby at that time. Most terminated at Lincoln. The Loop joined the East Lincolnshire main line at Bellwater Junction, where the 1913 25-lever signal box was still in use in 2015, although no longer serving a junction. (J.A.M.Vaughan)

4. Skegness Branch

SOUTH OF FIRSBY

80. This was the view from Firsby West signal box looking westward. A two-car DMU emerges from the single track spur from Skegness in April 1970. In the foreground is the direct double track line from Firsby to Boston. In the distant background is the curved Boston to Skegness line. The blind is incorrect as the destination is definitely not Skegness! (J.A.M.Vaughan)

81. No. 31275 is heading a typical holiday train on 28th July 1984. It is running from Sheffield to Skegness and is on the sharp curve at the bottom of map XVI, near picture 56. South Junction Box can be seen in picture 48 in *Spalding to Grimsby*. (J.Whitehouse)

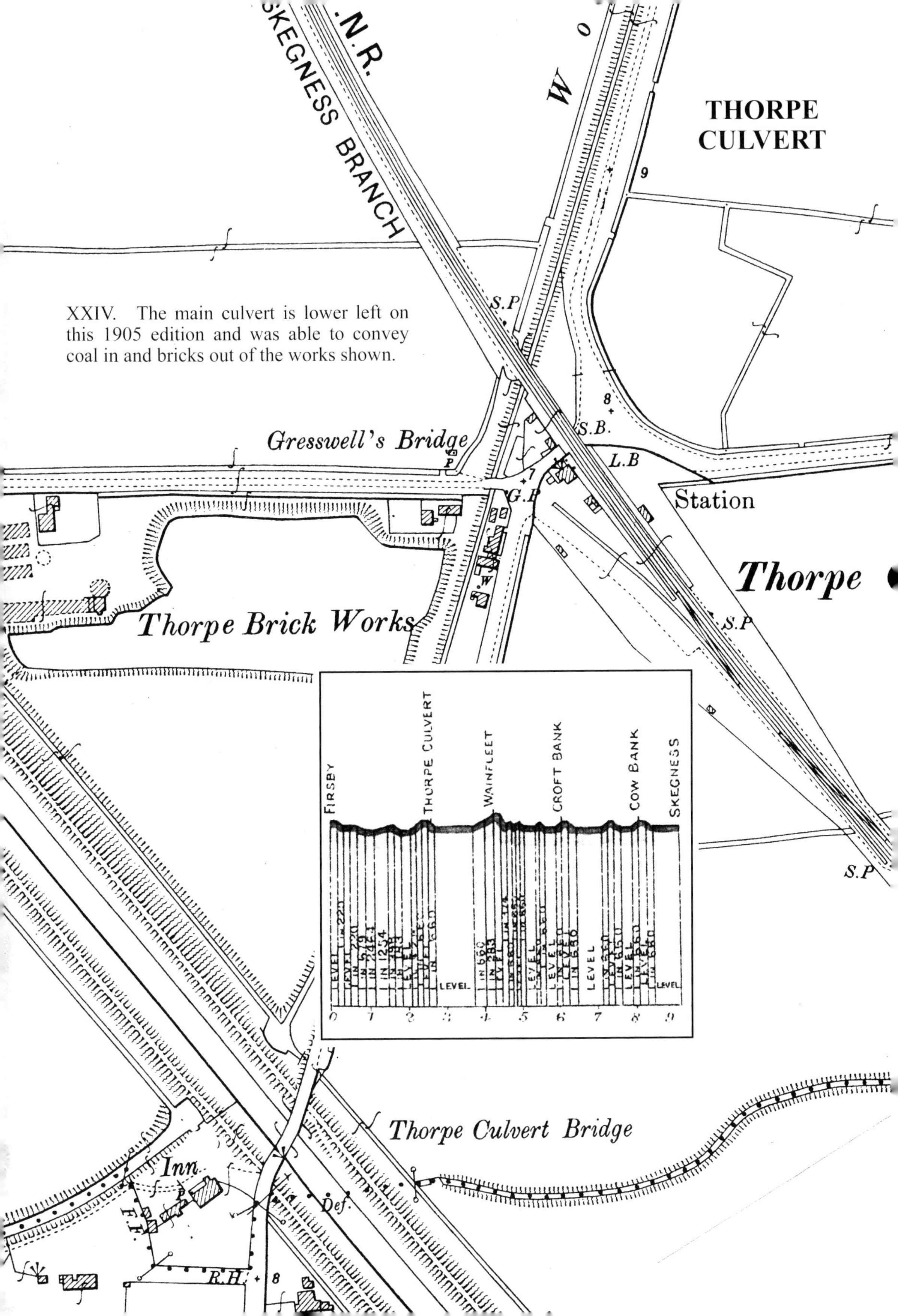

XXIV. The main culvert is lower left on this 1905 edition and was able to convey coal in and bricks out of the works shown.

82. We start with two pictures from the mid-1950s. On the left is part of the small goods yard, which was in use until 27th April 1964. Both platforms were listed for three coaches in 2006. (W.A.Camwell/SLS)

83. When DMUs were introduced in 1955, they were described by some admirers as the "cat's whiskers". They were initially painted with them, but soon "high vis" panels were required. Two designs of signal posts are evident. (W.A.Camwell/SLS)

84. Seen on 28th July 1984 is the 08.16 Leicester to Skegness composed of Mk I coaches, hauled by nos. 20160 and 20140. Some appreciative ears have been positioned outside the leading coach. (J.Whitehouse)

85. The station had become a request stop by the time this photograph was taken on 6th August 2015. No. 153321 is passing through, bound for Nottingham. (Janet Smith)

86. The signal box was totally rebuilt in 2003 and reopened on 2nd April. The original one had a 22-lever frame, but the one seen in 2015 had a panel instead. (Janet Smith)

WAINFLEET

XXV. Lower left is the Steeping River, which meanders to the right on this 1905 extract. It brought prosperity to the district before the coming of the railway. The corn mill was later incorporated into the brewery. This market town had for long been a port. The road name lower right is Haven Side.

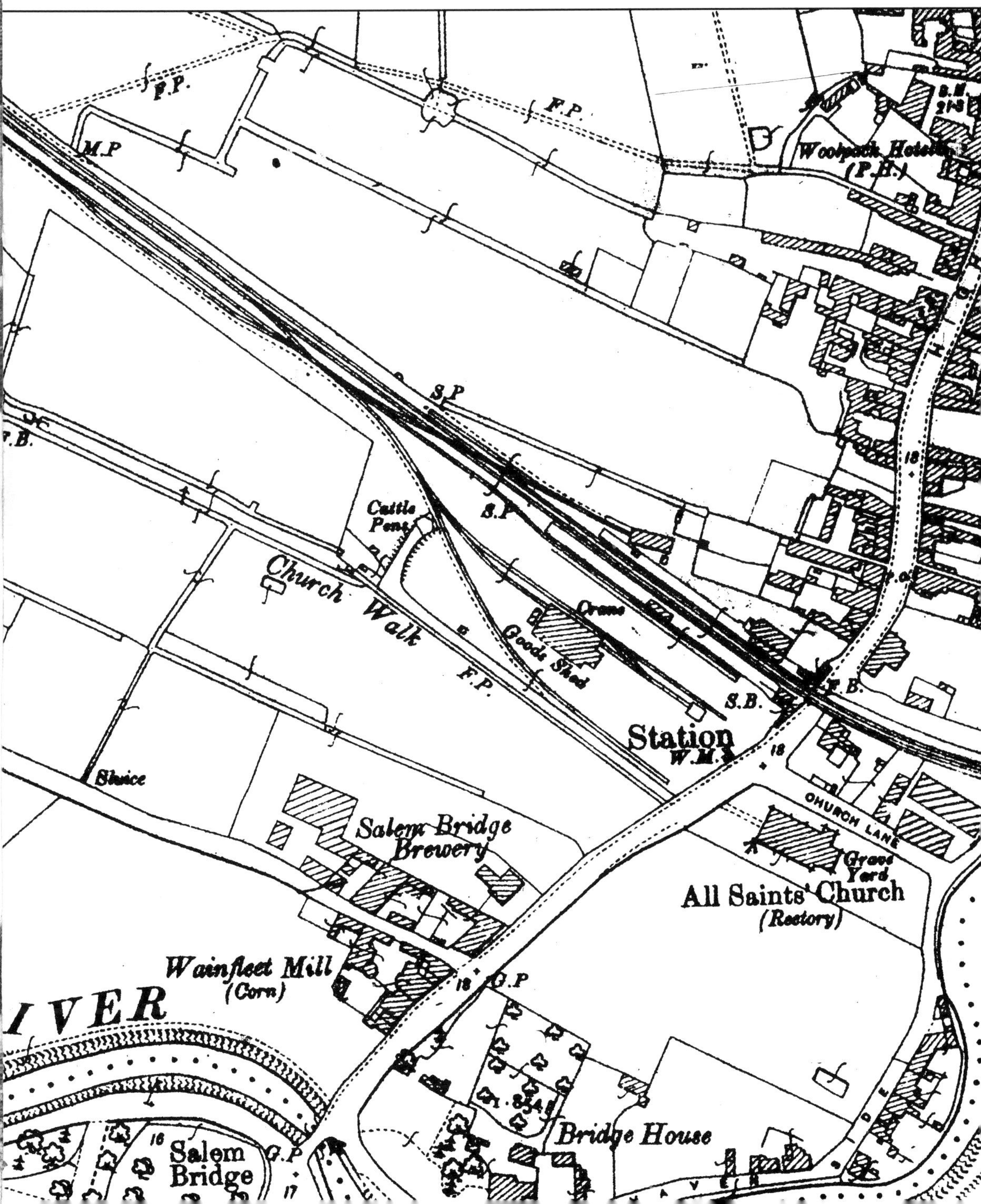

90. Departing in about 1965 is a DMU bound for Skegness. The canopy and footbridge were soon to vanish. Staffing ceased on 7th October 1968, except at the signal box. (Milepost 92½)

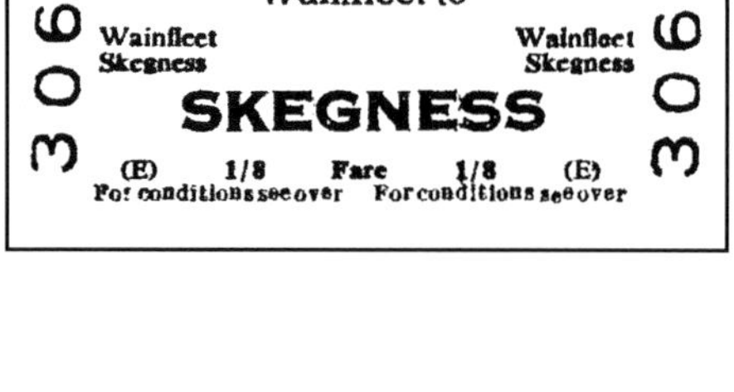

91. A class 101 DMU is leading the 11.30 Skegness to Nottingham on 28th July 1984. The only addition to the scene is a set of steps for use by the less mobile. (J.Whitehouse)

92. Sadly surrounded by weeds on 6th August 2015, the GNR signal box from about 1899 was still in use. Its frame had 25 levers. (Janet Smith)

93. We have two more photos from the same day. This one shows just two shelters for passengers, the main building having been railed off as a dwelling. (Janet Smith)

94. Half a mile to the east was Wainfleet Bypass Crossing, which was fitted with automatic half barriers. This is the 11.23 Skegness to Nottingham, worked by no. 153384. (Janet Smith)

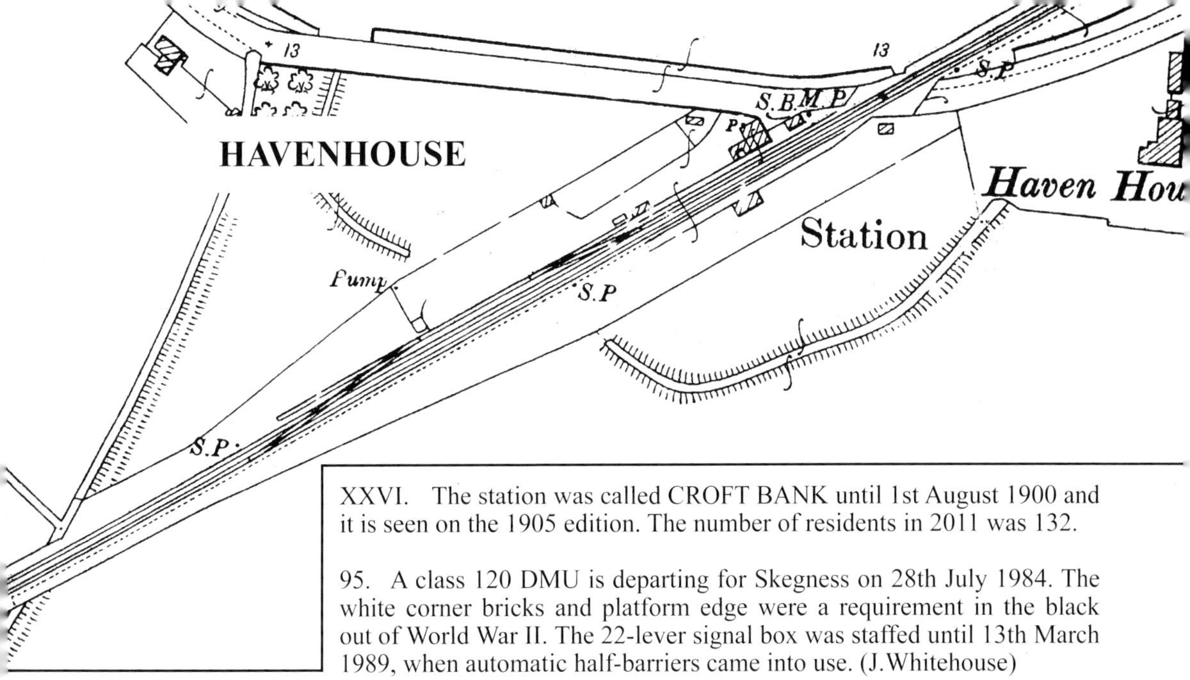

XXVI. The station was called CROFT BANK until 1st August 1900 and it is seen on the 1905 edition. The number of residents in 2011 was 132.

95. A class 120 DMU is departing for Skegness on 28th July 1984. The white corner bricks and platform edge were a requirement in the black out of World War II. The 22-lever signal box was staffed until 13th March 1989, when automatic half-barriers came into use. (J.Whitehouse)

96. We offer two more views from the same day. This features no. 40122 with the 08.15 Manchester Piccadilly to Skegness and the long single gate with a substantial tie bar. (J.Whitehouse)

97. No. 31422 is bound for Skegness, with the leading Mk I coach passing over the bridge above a stream. The goods yard had been behind the train until closure on 15th June 1964. (J.Whitehouse)

98. No. 156414 is working the 13.56 Skegness to Crewe service on 6th August 2003, although the trip would be cut short that day at Blythe Bridge. Old jointed track was still in use on many parts of the route. This platform took three cars, but on the down one only two were allowed. (A.C.Hartless)

99. A seat can be seen in the previous picture; in this one is the passenger shelter. The date is 6th August 2015 and at that time there were just two trains calling each way on weekdays and one on Sundays. (Janet Smith)

SEACROFT

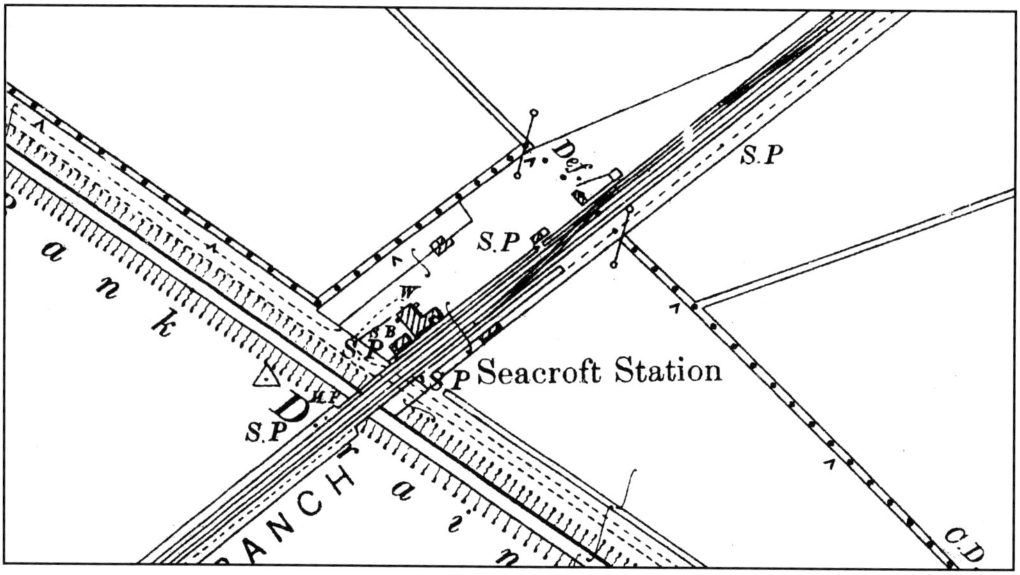

XXVII. The 1905 edition shows yet another station with its level crossing close to a fenland drain. The single goods siding was usable until 27th July 1964.

100. Here were the shortest platforms on the branch and they had early closure: 7th December 1953. The 1899 signal box had 22 levers and was reduced to a gate box on 19th December 1967, closure coming on 29th April 1990. The photo is from 1955. (Stations UK)

101. A 1964 view features the gates which were replaced by an automatic open crossing with monitor. In the distance is a Skegness gas holder. (Stations UK)

SKEGNESS

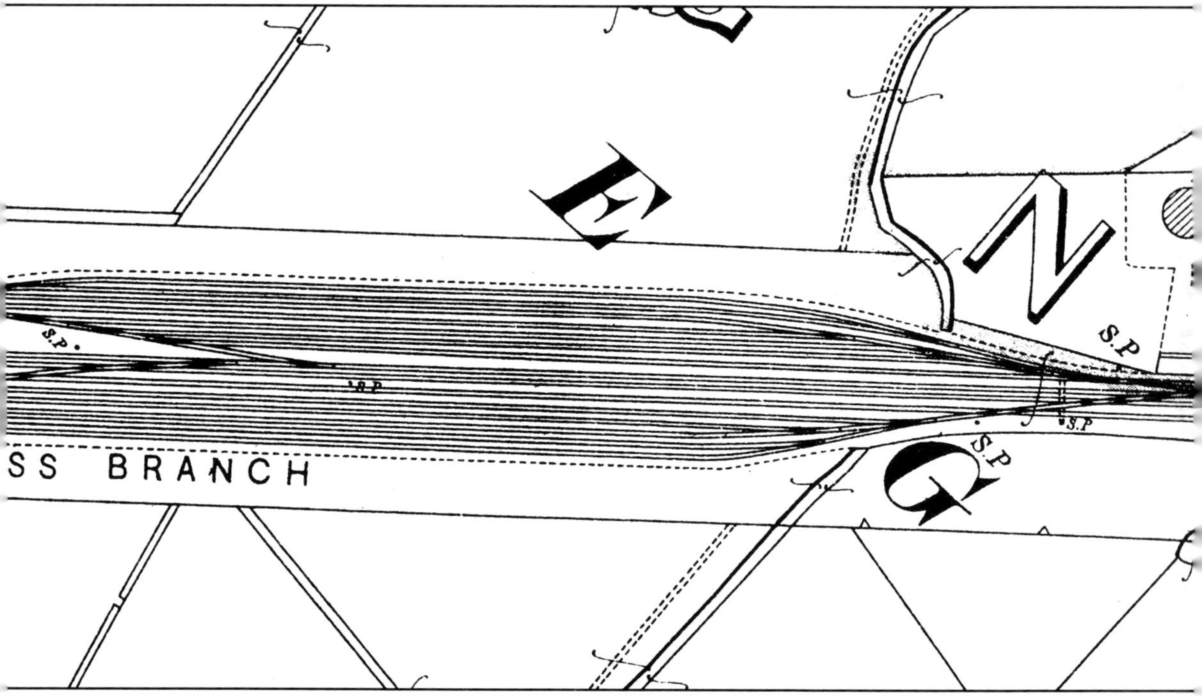

XXVIII. The two gas holders are on opposite pages. The Skegness Gas Light & Coke Co. was formed in 1878, but by 1900 was only using 600 tons of coal per annum. The U.D.C. took over in 1916. They carbonised 5985 tons in 1935 and through the 1950s took about 11,000 tons per annum.

102. The extensive buildings were completed two years after the railway opened in 1873. The location was to become known as the "Blackpool of the East" or "Nottingham-by-Sea". (P.Laming coll.)

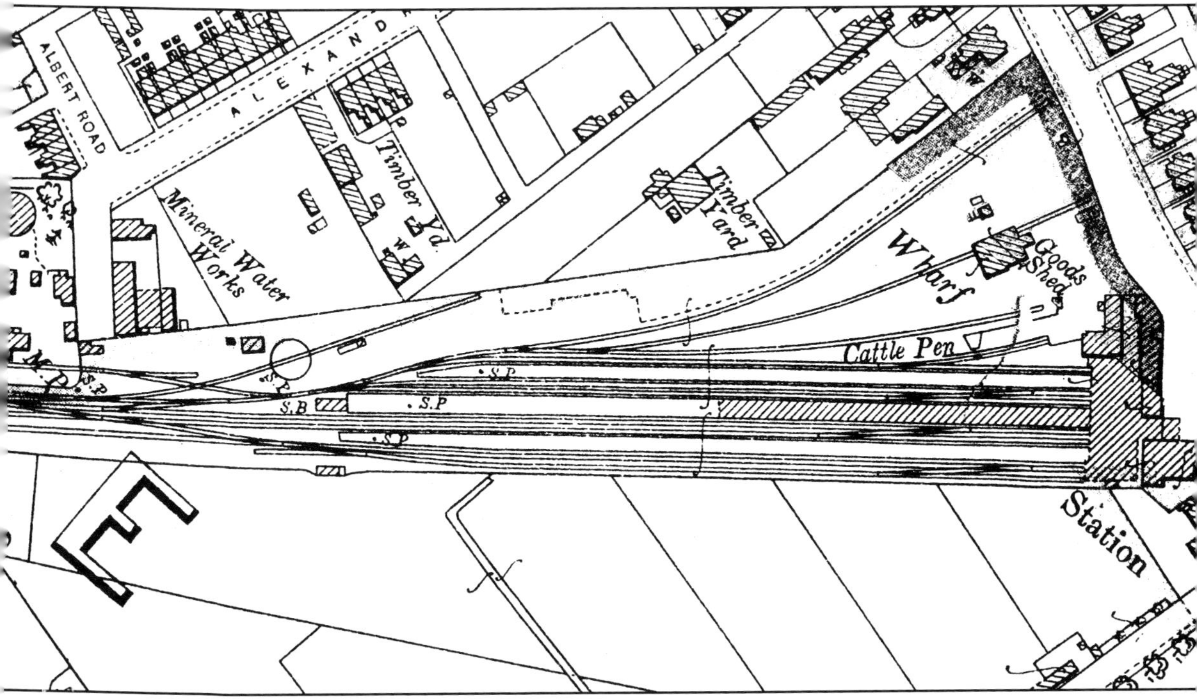

The works was in production until the mid-1960s. The map is from 1905 and has carriage sidings on the left page.

103. This postcard producer captioned this as "Arrival of London Excursion". A splendid tree-lined promenade, plus the Tower Gardens, had been created to attract the crowds. The population grew from 2140 in 1901 to 12,410 in 1961. (P.Laming coll.)

104. By the time of this 1933 photograph, the gasworks had just one massive holder capable of dealing with the enormous demand for a cooked breakfast. A local train arrives behind class D2 4-4-0 no. 4363. (R.S.Carpenter coll.)

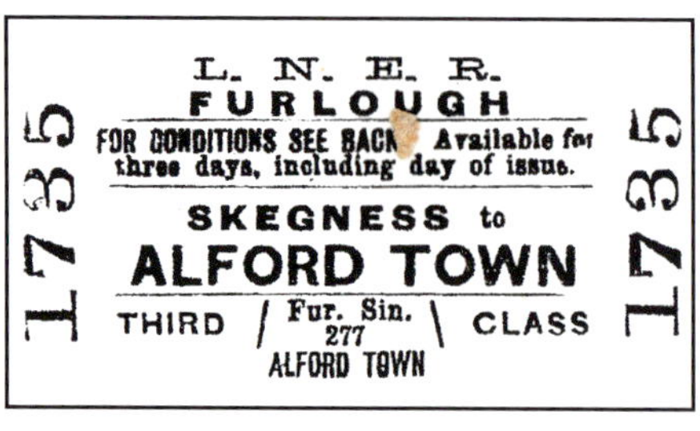

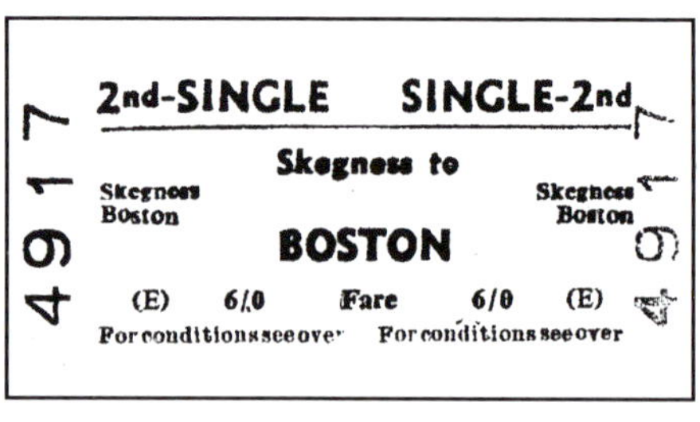

105. It is 29th April 1954 and class K2 2-6-0 no. 61757 is running between an ex-GNR somersault signal and the coal lift on the modernised retort house. Four fire buckets are to hand. (R.M.Casserley)

106. A 1955 view has reference to Butlin's Holiday Camp, which had been established at Skegness in 1936. It was an immense success and its capacity had to be doubled within a year. (Stations UK)

↑ 107. A panorama from 1954 gives an indication of the extent of the layout. The sidings on the right are being relaid. They had been laid in 1936-37 as additional carriage sidings for excursions. There was a turntable near the left border, but no engine shed. The table was 45ft 6ins in length and had a coal hoist nearby from 1936. The depot closed on 27th April 1966. (H.C.Casserley)

↓ 108. It is 1955 and this is the view from the signal box, but no details were recorded. Records from 1935 listed the average number of trains per day in May to be 93 and in August they numbered 126. (Stations UK)

109. Seen on 11th July 1969, a Derby Twin unit that had travelled from Lincoln on the 1913 "New Line" via Coningsby and Bellwater Junction rests at Platform 3. DMUs came to the line in 1957. (J.A.M.Vaughan)

110. This April 1970 view has a fence along the site of Platform 1. Beyond it stands the goods shed; the yard had closed on 2nd May 1966 and it became a car park. There had been a 5-ton crane available. (R.F.Roberts/SLS)

111. No. 37196 is at the head of an eight-coach train on 16th July 1983. A signal is off, although behind the driver. Another train is in Platform 7. (P.D.Shannon)

112. Skegness has always been noted for its holiday traffic, even in the diesel era. On 15th September 1984, class 20s nos. 20168 and 20054 leave the seaside terminus with the 11.58 to Leicester. Note the splendid array of semaphore signals, the smaller ones being for "calling on" only. (P.D.Shannon)

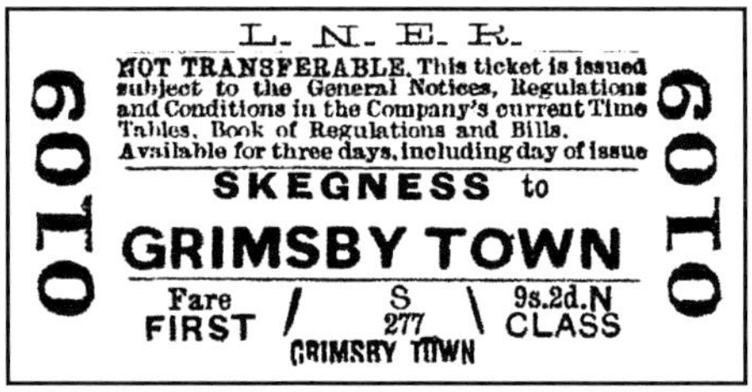

113. Two photographs from 22nd February 1978 reveal transitions without alterations. The impressive historic concourse was given over to cars of those wishing to leave Skegness. (D.A.Thompson)

114. The exterior was rather featureless. An HST arrived on 22nd February 1992 as part of a scheme to introduce the prestigious stock to the route, but poor track condition thwarted the plan. DMUs only became the rule. (D.A.Thompson)

115. The ornate signal box was fitted with an 80-lever frame and it was still in use in 2015. This and the next picture are from 3rd September 1988. The departing DMU was based at Tyseley, near Birmingham. To reduce overcrowding in 2007, Central Trains coupled 158 units to 157s to form 5-car sets, at peak times. Skegness had an electric tramway, but only in 1995-96. (J.Whitehouse)

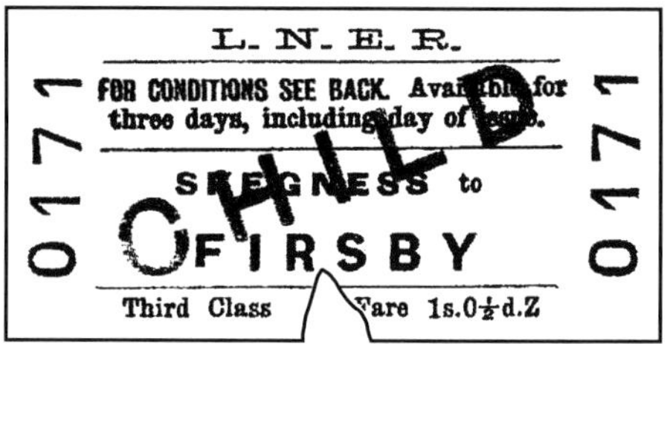

116. Under its shunt signal is no. 45106 propelling the empty stock of the 06.36 Sheffield to Skegness into one of the sidings. Merrymaker trains from King's Cross were introduced on 17th August 2006 for Summer Saturday excursions. The trains were limited to 30mph on the branch, due to poor track condition. The three remaining sidings were overgrown and deemed "Out of Use" since 1998. (J.Whitehouse)

117. In 1908, the town's mascot, the "Jolly Fisherman" was born. Designed by illustrator John Hassall, Jolly first appeared on a poster commissioned by the Great Northern Railway to promote its rail services. The poster depicted a cheery, somewhat rotund fellow smoking a pipe and the slogan "SKEGNESS is SO bracing". For 24 years the sculpture of the "Jolly Fisherman" by Sioban Coppinger stood on the station concourse; by 2011 it was in serious need of restoration. The cost of this being so high, the original sculptor was commissioned to create a replacement, which was incorporated into the station plaza in 2013. (Janet Smith)

118. The concourse was also photographed on 6th August 2015. The motor cars had long gone and redecoration had created an impressive environment and welcome sight for visitors. The platforms took 10 to 12 coaches each. (Janet Smith)

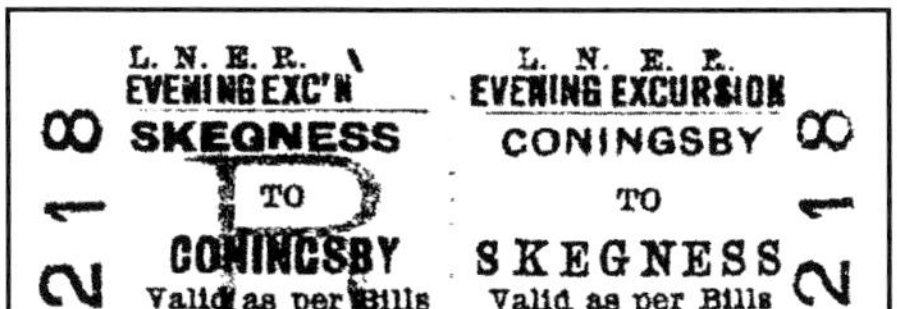

119. The historic building has been well conserved and feels authentic, with a functioning booking office and a refreshment room. More traditional seating could further enhance the ambience. (Janet Smith)

120. We end our survey by gazing at six terminal platforms and a manual signal box, all in working order on 26th September 2015. I had this pleasure and then returned on the 13.15, seen here, to Nottingham. Strongly recommended. (V.Mitchell)

MP Middleton Press

EVOLVING THE ULTIMATE RAIL ENCYCLOPEDIA

Easebourne Midhurst GU29 9AZ. Tel:01730 813169

www.middletonpress.co.uk email:info@middletonpress.co.uk

A-978 0 906520 B-978 1 873793 C-978 1 901706 D-978 1 904474
E-978 1 906008 F-978 1 908174

All titles listed below were in print at time of publication - please check current availability by looking at our website - *www.middletonpress.co.uk* or by requesting a Brochure which includes our *LATEST* RAILWAY TITLES also our TRAMWAY, TROLLEYBUS, MILITARY and COASTAL series

A
Abergavenny to Merthyr C 91 8
Abertillery & Ebbw Vale Lines D 84 5
Aberystwyth to Carmarthen E 90 1
Allhallows - Branch Line to A 62 8
Alton - Branch Lines to A 11 6
Andover to Southampton A 82 6
Ascot - Branch Lines around A 64 2
Ashburton - Branch Line to B 95 4
Ashford - Steam to Eurostar B 67 1
Ashford to Dover A 48 2
Austrian Narrow Gauge D 04 3
Avonmouth - BL around D 42 5
Aylesbury to Rugby D 91 3

B
Baker Street to Uxbridge D 90 6
Bala to Llandudno E 87 1
Banbury to Birmingham D 27 2
Banbury to Cheltenham E 63 5
Bangor to Holyhead F 01 7
Bangor to Portmadoc E 72 7
Barking to Southend C 80 2
Barmouth to Pwllheli E 53 6
Barry - Branch Lines around D 50 0
Bartlow - Branch Lines to F 27 7
Bath Green Park to Bristol C 36 9
Bath to Evercreech Junction A 60 4
Beamish 40 years on rails E94 9
Bedford to Wellingborough D 31 9
Berwick to Drem F 64 2
Berwick to St. Boswells F 75 8
B'ham to Tamworth & Nuneaton F 63 5
Birkenhead to West Kirby F 61 1
Birmingham to Wolverhampton E253
Bletchley to Cambridge D 94 4
Bletchley to Rugby E 07 9
Bodmin - Branch Lines around B 83 1
Boston to Lincoln F 80 2
Bournemouth to Evercreech Jn A 46 8
Bournemouth to Weymouth A 57 4
Bradshaw's History F18 5
Bradshaw's Rail Times 1850 F 13 0
Bradshaw's Rail Times 1895 F 11 6
Branch Lines series - see town names
Brecon to Neath D 43 2
Brecon to Newport D 16 6
Brecon to Newtown E 06 2
Brighton to Eastbourne A 16 1
Brighton to Worthing A 03 1
Bristol to Taunton D 03 6
Bromley South to Rochester B 23 7
Bromsgrove to Birmingham D 87 6
Bromsgrove to Gloucester D 73 9
Broxbourne to Cambridge F16 1
Brunel - A railtour D 74 6
Bude - Branch Line to B 29 9
Burnham to Evercreech Jn B 68 0

C
Cambridge to Ely D 55 5
Canterbury - BLs around B 58 9
Cardiff to Dowlais (Cae Harris) E 47 5
Cardiff to Pontypridd E 95 6
Cardiff to Swansea E 42 0
Carlisle to Hawick E 85 7
Carmarthen to Fishguard E 66 6
Caterham & Tattenham Corner B251
Central & Southern Spain NG E 91 8
Chard and Yeovil - BLs a C 30 7
Charing Cross to Dartford A 75 8
Charing Cross to Orpington A 96 3
Cheddar - Branch Line to B 90 9
Cheltenham to Andover C 43 7
Cheltenham to Redditch D 81 4
Chester to Birkenhead F 21 5
Chester to Manchester F 51 2
Chester to Rhyl E 93 2
Chester to Warrington F 40 6
Chichester to Portsmouth A 14 7
Clacton and Walton - BLs to F 04 8
Clapham Jn to Beckenham Jn B 36 7
Cleobury Mortimer - BLs a E 18 5
Clevedon & Portishead - BLs to D180
Consett to South Shields E 57 4
Cornwall Narrow Gauge D 56 2
Corris and Vale of Rheidol E 65 9
Craven Arms to Llandeilo E 35 2
Craven Arms to Wellington E 33 8
Crawley to Littlehampton A 34 5
Crewe to Manchester F 57 4
Cromer - Branch Lines around C 26 0
Croydon to East Grinstead B 48 0
Crystal Palace & Catford Loop B 87 1
Cyprus Narrow Gauge E 13 0

D
Darjeeling Revisited F 09 3
Darlington Leamside Newcastle E 28 4
Darlington to Newcastle D 98 2
Dartford to Sittingbourne B 34 3
Denbigh - Branch Lines around F 32 1
Derwent Valley - BL to the D 06 7
Devon Narrow Gauge E 09 3
Didcot to Banbury D 02 9
Didcot to Swindon C 84 0
Didcot to Winchester C 13 0
Dorset & Somerset NG D 76 0
Douglas - Laxey - Ramsey E 75 8
Douglas to Peel C 88 8
Douglas to Port Erin C 55 0
Douglas to Ramsey D 39 5
Dover to Ramsgate A 78 9
Dublin Northwards in 1950s E 31 4
Dunstable - Branch Lines to E 27 7

E
Ealing to Slough C 42 0
Eastbourne to Hastings A 27 7
East Cornwall Mineral Railways D 22 7
East Croydon to Three Bridges A 53 6
Eastern Spain Narrow Gauge E 56 7
East Grinstead - BLs to A 07 9
East London - Branch Lines of C 44 4
East London Line B 80 0
East of Norwich - Branch Lines E 69 7
Effingham Junction - BLs a A 74 1
Ely to Norwich C 90 1
Enfield Town & Palace Gates D 32 6
Epsom to Horsham A 30 7
Eritrean Narrow Gauge E 38 3
Euston to Harrow & Wealdstone C 89 5
Exeter to Barnstaple B 15 2
Exeter to Newton Abbot C 49 9
Exeter to Tavistock B 69 5
Exmouth - Branch Lines to B 00 8

F
Fairford - Branch Line to A 52 9
Falmouth, Helston & St. Ives C 74 1
Fareham to Salisbury A 67 3
Faversham to Dover B 05 3
Felixstowe & Aldeburgh - BL to D 20 3
Fenchurch Street to Barking C 20 8
Festiniog - 50 yrs of enterprise C 83 3
Festiniog 1946-55 E 01 7
Festiniog in the Fifties B 68 8
Festiniog in the Sixties B 91 6
Ffestiniog in Colour 1955-82 F 25 3
Finsbury Park to Alexandra Pal C 02 8
Frome to Bristol B 77 0

G
Galashiels to Edinburgh F 52 9
Gloucester to Bristol D 35 7
Gloucester to Cardiff D 66 1
Gosport - Branch Lines around A 36 9
Greece Narrow Gauge D 72 2

H
Hampshire Narrow Gauge D 36 4
Harrow to Watford D 14 2
Harwich & Hadleigh - BLs to F 02 4
Harz Revisited F 62 8
Hastings to Ashford A 37 6
Hawick to Galashiels F 36 9
Hawkhurst - Branch Line to A 66 6
Hayling - Branch Line to A 12 3
Hay-on-Wye - BL around D 92 0
Haywards Heath to Seaford A 28 4
Hemel Hempstead - BLs to D 88 3
Henley, Windsor & Marlow - BLa C77 2
Hereford to Newport D 54 8
Hertford & Hatfield - BLs a E 58 1
Hertford Loop E 71 0
Hexham to Carlisle D 75 3
Hexham to Hawick F 08 6
Hitchin to Peterborough D 07 4
Holborn Viaduct to Lewisham A 81 9
Horsham - Branch Lines to A 02 4
Huntingdon - Branch Line to A 93 2

I
Ilford to Shenfield C 97 0
Ilfracombe - Branch Line to B 21 3
Industrial Rlys of the South East A 09 3
Ipswich to Diss F 81 9
Ipswich to Saxmundham C 41 3
Isle of Wight Lines - 50 yrs C 12 3
Italy Narrow Gauge F 17 8

K
Kent Narrow Gauge C 45 1
Kettering to Nottingham F 82-6
Kidderminster to Shrewsbury E 10 9
Kingsbridge - Branch Line to C 98 7
Kings Cross to Potters Bar E 62 8
King's Lynn to Hunstanton F 58 1
Kingston & Hounslow Loops A 83 3
Kingswear - Branch Line to C 17 8

L
Lambourn - Branch Line to C 70 3
Launceston & Princetown - BLs C 19 2
Lewisham to Dartford A 92 5
Lincoln to Cleethorpes F 56 7
Lines around Wimbledon B 75 6
Liverpool Street to Chingford D 01 2
Liverpool Street to Ilford C 34 5
Llandeilo to Swansea E 46 8
London Bridge to Addiscombe B 20 6
London Bridge to East Croydon A 58 1
Longmoor - Branch Lines to A 41 3
Looe - Branch Line to C 22 2
Loughborough to Nottingham F 68 0
Lowestoft - BLs around E 40 6
Ludlow to Hereford E 14 7
Lydney - Branch Lines around E 26 0
Lyme Regis - Branch Line to A 45 1
Lynton - Branch Line to B 04 6

M
Machynlleth to Barmouth E 54 3
Maesteg and Tondu Lines E 06 2
Majorca & Corsica Narrow Gauge F 41 3
March - Branch Lines around B 09 1
Market Drayton - BLs around F 67 3
Marylebone to Rickmansworth D 49 4
Melton Constable to Yarmouth Bch E031
Midhurst - Branch Lines of E 78 9
Midhurst - Branch Lines to F 00 0
Minehead - Branch Line to A 80 2
Mitcham Junction Lines B 01 5
Monmouth - Branch Lines to E 20 8
Monmouthshire Eastern Valleys D 71 5
Moretonhampstead - BL to C 27 7
Moreton-in-Marsh to Worcester D 26 5
Mountain Ash to Neath D 80 7

N
Newark to Doncaster F 78 9
Newbury to Westbury C 66 6
Newcastle to Hexham D 69 2
Newport (IOW) - Branch Lines to A 26 0
Newquay - Branch Lines to C 71 0
Newton Abbot to Plymouth C 60 4
Newtown to Aberystwyth E 41 3
North East German NG D 44 9
Northern Alpine Narrow Gauge F 37 6
Northern France Narrow Gauge C 75 8
Northern Spain Narrow Gauge E 83 3
North London Line B 94 7
North of Birmingham F 55 0
North Woolwich - BLs around C 65 9
Nottingham to Boston F 70 3
Nottingham to Lincoln F 43 7

O
Ongar - Branch Line to E 05 5
Orpington to Tonbridge B 03 9
Oswestry - Branch Lines around E 60 4
Oswestry to Whitchurch E 81 9
Oxford to Bletchley D 57 9
Oxford to Moreton-in-Marsh D 15 9

P
Paddington to Ealing C 37 6
Paddington to Princes Risborough C819
Padstow - Branch Line to B 54 1
Pembroke and Cardigan - BLs to F 29 1
Peterborough to Kings Lynn E 32 1
Peterborough to Newark F 72 7
Plymouth - BLs around B 98 5
Plymouth to St. Austell C 63 5
Pontypool to Mountain Ash D 65 4
Pontypridd to Merthyr F 14 7
Pontypridd to Port Talbot E 86 4
Porthmadog 1954-94 - BLa B 31 2
Portmadoc 1923-46 - BLa B 13 8
Portsmouth to Southampton A 31 4
Portugal Narrow Gauge E 67 3
Potters Bar to Cambridge D 70 8
Princes Risborough - BL to D 05 0
Princes Risborough to Banbury C 85 7

R
Railways to Victory C 16 1
Reading to Basingstoke B 27 5
Reading to Didcot C 79 6
Reading to Guildford A 47 5
Redhill to Ashford A 73 4
Return to Blaenau 1970-82 C 64 2
Rhyl to Bangor F 15 4
Rhymney & New Tredegar Lines E 48 2
Rickmansworth to Aylesbury D 61 6
Romania & Bulgaria NG E 23 9
Romneyrail C 32 1
Ross-on-Wye - BLs around E 30 7
Ruabon to Barmouth E 84 0
Rugby to Birmingham E 37 6
Rugby to Loughborough F 12 3
Rugby to Stafford F 07 9
Ryde to Ventnor A 19 2

S
Salisbury to Westbury B 39 8
Sardinia and Sicily Narrow Gauge F 50 5
Saxmundham to Yarmouth C 69 7
Saxony & Baltic Germany Revisited F 71 0
Saxony Narrow Gauge D 47 0
Seaton & Sidmouth - BLs to A 95 6
Selsey - Branch Line to A 04 8
Sheerness - Branch Line to B 16 2
Shenfield to Ipswich E 96 3
Shrewsbury - Branch Line to A 86 4
Shrewsbury to Chester E 70 3
Shrewsbury to Crewe F 48 2
Shrewsbury to Ludlow E 21 5
Shrewsbury to Newtown E 29 1
Sierra Leone Narrow Gauge D 28 9
Sirhowy Valley Line E 12 3
Sittingbourne to Ramsgate A 90 1
Skegness & Mablethorpe - BL to F 84 0
Slough to Newbury C 56 7
South African Two-foot gauge E 51 2
Southampton to Bournemouth A 42 0
Southend & Southminster BLs E 76 5
Southern Alpine Narrow Gauge F 22 2
Southern France Narrow Gauge C 47 5
South London Line B 46 6
South Lynn to Norwich City F 03 1
Southwold - Branch Line to A 15 4
Spalding - Branch Lines around E 52 9
Spalding to Grimsby F 65 9 6
Stafford to Chester F 34 5
Stafford to Wellington F 59 8
St Albans to Bedford D 08 1
St. Austell to Penzance C 67 3
St. Boswell to Berwick F 44 4
Steaming Through Isle of Wight A 56 7
Steaming Through West Hants A 69 7
Stourbridge to Wolverhampton E 16 1
St. Pancras to Barking D 68 5
St. Pancras to Folkestone E 88 8
St. Pancras to St. Albans C 78 9
Stratford to Cheshunt F 53 6
Stratford-u-Avon to Birmingham D777
Stratford-u-Avon to Cheltenham C253
Sudbury - Branch Lines to F 19 2
Surrey Narrow Gauge C 87 1
Sussex Narrow Gauge C 68 0
Swanley to Ashford B 45 9
Swansea - Branch Lines around F 38 3
Swansea to Carmarthen E 59 8
Swindon to Bristol C 96 3
Swindon to Gloucester D 46 3
Swindon to Newport D 30 2
Swiss Narrow Gauge C 94 9

T
Talyllyn 60 E 98 7
Tamworth to Derby F 76 5
Taunton to Barnstaple B 60 2
Taunton to Exeter C 82 6
Taunton to Minehead F 39 0
Tavistock to Plymouth B 88 6
Tenterden - Branch Line to A 21 5
Three Bridges to Brighton A 35 2
Tilbury Loop C 86 4
Tiverton - BLs around C 62 8
Tivetshall to Beccles D 41 8
Tonbridge to Hastings A 44 4
Torrington - Branch Lines to B 37 4
Towcester - BLs around E 39 0
Tunbridge Wells BLs A 32 1

U
Upwell - Branch Line to B 64 0

V
Victoria to Bromley South A 98 7
Victoria to East Croydon A 40 6
Vivarais Revisited E 08 6

W
Walsall Routes F 45 1
Wantage - Branch Line to D 25 8
Wareham to Swanage 50 yrs D098
Waterloo to Windsor A 54 3
Waterloo to Woking A 38 3
Watford to Leighton Buzzard D 45 6
Wellingborough to Leicester F 73 4
Welshpool to Llanfair E 49 9
Wenford Bridge to Fowey C 09 3
Westbury to Bath B 55 8
Westbury to Taunton C 76 5
West Cornwall Mineral Rlys D 48 7
West Croydon to Epsom B 08 4
West German Narrow Gauge D 93 7
West London - BLs of C 50 5
West London Line B 84 8
West Wiltshire - BLs of D 12 8
Weymouth - BLs A 65 9
Willesden Jn to Richmond B 71 8
Wimbledon to Beckenham C 58 1
Wimbledon to Epsom B 62 6
Wimborne - BLs around A 97 0
Wisbech - BLs around C 01 7
Witham & Kelvedon - BLs a E 82 6
Woking to Alton A 59 8
Woking to Portsmouth A 25 3
Woking to Southampton A 55 0
Wolverhampton to Shrewsbury E444
Wolverhampton to Stafford F 79 6
Worcester to Birmingham D 97 5
Worcester to Hereford D 38 8
Worthing to Chichester A 06 2
Wrexham to New Brighton F 47 5
Wroxham - BLs around F 31 4

Y
Yeovil - 50 yrs change C 38 3
Yeovil to Dorchester A 76 5
Yeovil to Exeter A 91 8
York to Scarborough F 23 9